Understanding the Nursery School

David Hartley

CASSELL

Cassell

Villiers House
41/47 Strand
London WC2N 5JE, England

387 Park Avenue South
New York
NY 10016–8810, USA

First published 1993

British Library Cataloguing-in-Publication Data
A catalogue record for this book is available from the British Library.

ISBN 0-304-32597-X (hardback)
     0-304-32584-8 (paperback)

Typeset by Colset Private Limited, Singapore
Printed and bound in Great Britain by
Biddles Ltd, Guildford and King's Lynn

Children, Teachers and Learning Series

Series Editor: Cedric Cullingford

Understanding the Nursery School

Contents

Foreword

The books in this series stem from the conviction that all those who are concerned with education should have a deep interest in the nature of children's learning. Teaching and policy decisions ultimately depend on an understanding of individual personalities accumulated through experience, observation and research. Too often in recent years decisions on the management of education have had little to do with the realities of children's lives, and too often the interest shown in the performance of teachers, or in the content of the curriculum, has not been balanced by an interest in how children respond to either. The books in this series are based on the conviction that children are not fundamentally different from adults, and that we understand ourselves better by our insight into the nature of children.

The books are designed to appeal to *all* those who are interested in education and who take it as axiomatic that anyone concerned with human nature, culture or the future of civilization is interested in education — in the individual process of learning, as well as what can be done to help it. While each book draws on recent findings in research and is aware of the latest developments in policy, each is written in a style that is clear, readable and free from the jargon that has undermined much scholarly writing, especially in such a relatively new field of study.

Although the audience to be addressed includes all those concerned with education, the most important section of the audience is made up of professional teachers, the teachers who continue to learn and grow and who need both support and stimulation. Teachers are very busy people, whose energies are taken up in coping with difficult circumstances. They deserve material that is stimulating, useful and free of jargon and that is in tune with the practical realities of classrooms.

Each book is based on the principle that the study of education is a discipline in its own right. There was a time when the study of the principles of learning and the individual's response to his or her environment was a collection of parts of other disciplines — history, philosophy, linguistics, sociology and psychology. That time is assumed to be over and the books address those who are interested in the study of children and how they respond to their environment.

Each book is written both to enlighten the readers and to offer practical help to develop their understanding. They therefore not only contain accounts of what we understand about children, but also illuminate these accounts by a series of examples, based on observation of practice. These examples are designed not as a series of rigid steps to be followed, but to show the realities on which the insights are based.

Most people, even educational researchers, agree that research on children's learning has been most disappointing, even when it has not been completely missing. Apart from the general lack of a 'scholarly' educational tradition, the inadequacies of such study come about because of the fear of approaching such a complex area as children's inner lives. Instead of answering curiosity with obser-vation, much educational research has attempted to reduce the problem to simplistic solutions, by isolating a particular hypothesis and trying to improve it, or by trying to focus on what is easy and 'empirical'. These books try to clarify the real complexities of the problem, and are willing to be speculative.

The real disappointment with educational research, however, is that it is very rarely read or used. The people most at home with children are often unaware that helpful insights can be offered to them. The study of children and the understanding that comes from self-knowledge are too important to be left to obscurity. In the broad sense real 'research' is carried out by all those engaged in the task of teaching or bringing up children.

All the books share a conviction that the inner worlds of children repay close attention, and that much subsequent behaviour and attitudes depend upon the early years. They also share the convic-tion that children's natures are not markedly different from those of adults, even if they are more honest about themselves. The process of learning is reviewed as the individual's close and idiosyncratic involvement in events, rather than the passive recep-tion of, and processing of, information.

Cedric Cullingford

CHAPTER 1
Introduction

Although most of us would not claim to be bureaucrats, we operate daily without much reflection in bureaucracies. In a modern, complex industrial society, it is difficult to escape from this type of organizational form. For many, the term 'bureaucracy' has a pejorative connotation, for it is said to tie us up in red tape, or treat us impersonally, referring to us by number, not name. When we criticize bureaucracy we probably have in mind its rigid manifestations of hierarchy, rules, routines and filing cabinets, and its standardization of time, space and behaviour. This view of bureaucracy associates with Max Weber's classic definition of the 'pure' bureaucracy during the age of factory-based manufacturing industry.

The face of bureaucracy is changing. It is said to have become 'looser', 'softer', more flexible and open, less hierarchical and more collegial in its style of decision-making. 'Top-down' control is giving way to 'bottom-up' control. What this metaphor means is that some workers now seem to control themselves rather than comply with the detailed directives passed down by officialdom. Notions of flexi-time and open-plan offices are indicative of the practice. Rather than being obviously managed, the worker, so to say, manages him or herself: some call it 'introspective management', a procedure aided and abetted by the ubiquitous Filofax and the watch that bleeps. Self-management and time-management replace the overseer and the factory hooter. And this bureaucratic cognitive style, as Peter Berger calls it, is not confined to our place of work: that is, it seeps across into our places of pleasure and leisure. For example, we might feel guilty if we fail to complete our leisure pursuits on time, or perhaps we set our watches to bleep every hour, on the hour. Put another way, the new form of bureaucracy requires us to control ourselves, rather than allow superiors to control us, as had been the case hitherto. And whereas before we had been publicly blamed, now we have a sense of private guilt.

1

What has all of this to do with childhood and schooling? Just as the bureaucratic form has become less rigid in the world of work, so too are there signs that the bureaucratic form of the school has loosened. The days of strict management regimes at work are fast abating, as are the classrooms of serried ranks and corporal punishment. The definition of childhood has also shifted. What counted as childhood at the turn of the century may not be appropriate today. The new work-based form of bureaucracy requires of schools a new pedagogy which will prepare the psychology of the child for it. However, this suggests a goodness of fit between the form of the school and the social structure of the workplace. This itself implies a level of passivity in schools which is too extreme: those who work in schools will interpret the forces for change beyond them in ways not always predictable.

The focus of this book is mainly on the relationship between the dominant societal form of organization, namely bureaucracy, and what counts as childhood. In particular, we shall be concerned with the two years before compulsory schooling, and with the institution which leads up to it, namely the nursery school. What is interesting about some nursery schools is that they are institutions which purport not to be institutions: that is, they try to allow the children to *be themselves*, free of institutional constraints. To take this view is to share the romantic view of the child held by Rousseau. Other nursery schools may take a different view, perhaps regarding the purpose of nursery education as a more formal preparation for primary school, equipping the child with the rudiments of language, number and appropriate behaviour. Thus nursery education means different things to different people. My impression, after having talked to nursery educators, is that their views incorporate the moral philosophy of Rousseau and the developmental psychology of Piaget, especially the latter. Also prominent, particularly in state-funded nurseries in deprived areas, is a quest to compensate children for the deprivation of their domestic circumstances, a tradition which goes back to the pioneering work of the McMillan sisters. The influence of bureaucratic rationality does not seem to be part of the professional vocabulary of infant educators: that is, it does not form part of their explanations of what it is they do. But the bureaucratic form of contemporary society exists, and how it affects nursery education is central to this book. I wish to emphasize that whenever the term 'bureaucratic' is used, no evaluative connotation, pejorative or laudatory, is implied. I am using the term 'bureaucracy' as a concept for analytical purposes only.

My concern is *not* to do with either the content of curriculum or with cognitive psychology. Nor does it focus on matters of attainment in language and number, or with the academic effects of early education. (These have been fully dealt with in the compensatory education literature, and more recently by Tizard *et al.* and Osborn and Milbank.[1]) Rather, it is more to do with the hidden curriculum of nursery schools. In this respect, the book is different from much other research on early education and primary education. My approach will be sociological, drawing upon the historical sociology of Norbert Elias and the methodology of non-participant observation. It is written with the nursery or primary teacher in mind, both teachers in practice and those in training. Professionals involved in aspects of child care, especially social workers, may find the study relevant. No intention to be prescriptive is meant. I hope to suggest that the differing interpretations of childhood and nursery education which the study generates can be understood more in relation to social structural considerations than by appeals to theory in psychology. By so doing, I shall try to move the focus away from 'the child' to 'the child in society'. As is normal in such studies, I have preserved the anonymity of children and staff, as well as the names and locations of the schools.

The structure of the book is as follows. The study is located historically by analysing the evolution of the cultural definition of childhood since the Middle Ages. This analysis is informed by the theory of the civilizing process propounded by Norbert Elias. It sees childhood as being influenced by movements in Western civilization, among them being romanticism, Protestantism, capitalism, Darwinism and empirical science. But central to the development of what counts as childhood is Elias's insight that childhood, as a cultural category, developed as Western civilization acquired a sense of embarrassment and shame. Inserted into this historical analysis will be the three nursery schools: their catchment areas, formal goals and composition. In Chapter 3, we shall begin the empirical part of the study, and we shall filter the events within the nurseries through the concept of bureau-cracy. Specifically, we shall consider how time, space and activi-ties are all structured within each nursery, noting the variations between them, and attempting to explain those variations socio-logically. In Chapter 5 we shall consider how the nurseries try to reconcile a contradiction: that is, how can they retain the innocence and freedom of the individual child in an age which bears witness to an ever-expanding institutionalization and standardization of society? Finally, we attend to the staff of the nurseries, both teachers and nursery nurses. Are, for example, their professional views shared? In what ways are their practices influenced by the social structure of which they are a part? In the explanation of what they say and do, are they more likely to invoke theory from developmental psychology and moral philosophy than to draw insights from history and social theory? Finally, we turn to the immediate future which might beset early education, a domain of education which hitherto has largely been set aside in policy analyses, but which now seems set to attract policy review.

NOTES AND REFERENCES

1. Tizard, B., Blatchford, P., Burke, J., Farquhar, C. and Plewis, I. *Young Children at School in the Inner City*. Hove: Lawrence Erlbaum Associates, 1988; and Osborn, A. F. and Milbank, J. E. *The Effects of Early Education: A Report from the Child Health Education Study*. Oxford: Oxford University Press, 1987.

CHAPTER 2

Childhood and Society

In the study of early education, it is common to draw upon the theoretical insights of psychology. There are two reasons for this: first it is through the scientific discourse of psychology, particularly developmental psychology, that our understanding of child development is said to be furthered; and second, it follows that once we understand the nature of the child in this way, then certain pedagogical practices suggest themselves. In this chapter, these two considerations are discussed from a sociohistorical standpoint. That is to say, we shall firstly regard childhood not as a fixed set of basic attributes, but as an outcome of sociological trends in Western civilization. Second, the discipline of psychology itself, especially psychometry and developmental psychology, will be interpreted through this same sociohistorical framework. Specifically, the analysis covers the following: an introductory comment on the general relationship between educational ideas and society; the social structuring of childhood since the Middle Ages, drawing upon the sociology of Norbert Elias; the emergence of psychology and its consequences for childhood and pedagogy; and finally the relationship between changes in class structure and the forms of pedagogy, drawing on the work of Bernstein.[1] This wide-ranging approach within so limited a space will permit no more than an analytical gloss. Nevertheless the analysis may go some way to providing those involved in nursery and primary education with a wider view of their everyday professional practice. It will offer a framework with which to interpret the events in the three nursery schools which are to be reported in later chapters.

Educational concepts and social structure

The world of objects and events has no inherent meaning. These are apprehended by us through our senses, but they do not, so

5

to say, speak for themselves. We must assign meaning to them. So, when we see and hear children going about their lives in a nursery school, various meanings may be assigned to these events. What are they doing and why are they doing it? Are they, for example, getting ready for primary school? Are they just playing? Are they merely being cared for while their parents are at work? To the average onlooker, all this may be so much a part of normal, everyday life that it seems superfluous even to ask what it all means. It happens everywhere. It is the way things are.

A profession has a repertoire of concepts with which it interprets its clients. Given these interpretations, decisions are then made about how the client shall be treated. These concepts, although they exist only at the level of ideas, may claim to have objective, real status. Put another way, the concepts become reified. Take, for example, the concept of *school*. This concept not only has an architectural and physical association, thereby giving it real substance, but it also has social and political connotations: that is, it is a place where individuals are assembled, organized and taught this or that curriculum by means of this or that pedagogy. Some concepts in education cannot so easily be given substance, but nevertheless they acquire a status which *superficially* appears to be substantive. An example is the concept of *intelligence*.[2] Its claim to objective status turns on the use of the IQ test and the statistical artefact of the normal curve of distribution. Because IQ test scores produce a normal curve, rather like the distribution of biological characteristics such as eye-colour or height, it has been claimed that what these tests measure, namely 'intelligence', must surely have an objective, natural and biological quality. But even if it were possible to accept these statistical procedures, there remain the unanswered questions of which knowledge from a culture shall comprise the IQ tests, and of who should select it. All this is quite apart from the wider question of why, in the first place, we should suddenly start testing children on a grand scale, and why we are so concerned with both racial and social class differences in IQ scores.

Consider a further educational concept: *curriculum*. Here the matter touched on in relation to the concept of intelligence (that is, the matter of who shall define it, and why) looms larger.

What shall children know, and, more importantly, what shall they remain ignorant of? It is currently fashionable among pro-business politicians to make schooling and curriculum 'relevant to the real world'. In effect this means *their* definition of real, namely, the interests of employers. At other times, different considerations have been applied to decisions about the curriculum. For example, the nineteenth-century aristocracy had no truck with a so-called vocational education for their sons, simply because they had no need of a vocation. And even if it is decided to teach a subject, such as history, there remain important questions to answer about the interpretation to place on historical 'facts', or indeed which facts to include or exclude. For example, do we regard the pacification of the North American Indian as a civilizing process, or as genocide? Do we interpret the use of young children in the mines and factories of nineteenth-century industrial Britain as economic development or as the enslavement and degradation of a nation's children?

Of all commonplace educational concepts, that of 'the child' seems to be the least problematic, the most clear-cut. Its objectivity as a concept and category turns on the fact that physically the child has not fully developed. In that biological sense children are different from adults. Whereas there is much confusion about what counts as, say, 'intelligence', there is less about what shall constitute the child *in the physical sense*. This physical objectivity of the child has consequences for the psychology of childhood: that is, the child has been abstracted from its social context as the unit of analysis in psychological theory. Childhood, however, is not the fixed entity that some psychological theory might deem it to be. What counts as childhood varies.

It may even be on the way out. Postman has made the incisive point that whenever historians begin to focus upon a phenomenon we can suspect that it is fast disappearing.[3] Since the publication of Aries's *Centuries of Childhood* in 1962 there has been a spate of work on the history of childhood, among the most prominent of which are Linda Pollock's *Forgotten Children* and *Constructing and Reconstructing Childhood*, edited by James and Prout.[4] It is Postman's argument that childhood is disappearing: that is, there are fewer and fewer distinctions which may be made at the cultural level between adults and children.[5] To state some of

7

Postman's points: children's sport is becoming professionalized; cosmetics and fashions are becoming shared by children and adults; through both television and videos, adults and children have access to each other's entertainment; what the Opies called the traditional 'lore and language' of children is little in evidence.[6] In a related analysis, Meyrowitz notes how the age of the printing press enabled adults to distance themselves from children.[7] In an oral culture, children could interact with adults; in a 'print' culture they could not, unless they were schooled. Today, however, children again have access to adult worlds through television even before they learn to read and write. To summarize Meyrowitz: '[school] cannot assume that even children in the early grades will be willing to accept the idealized and mythologized versions of reality that were designed for "innocent children" '.[8] To all of this must be added the demographic trend that fewer children are being born, and, when they are, parents seem less willing to spend time with them. Even the traditional bedtime story can be safely entrusted to British Telecom or Bell Telephone. In short, children are physically different from adults, but the central question to be asked here is: *What meanings has the culture assigned to that difference?* It will be suggested that, in historical terms, childhood seems to be a recent phenomenon. (I say 'seems' to be a recent historical phenomenon because, as Pollock reminds us, the historical record is mainly of secondary sources.) The argument here is that what required its introduction as an age of 'innocence' was an increasing sense of shame in Western civilization. In order to develop this it is necessary to turn to Elias's sociological theory.

Social structure and childhood since the Middle Ages: the sociology of Norbert Elias

Norbert Elias was born in Breslau in 1897, the son of a physician. After deciding that his father's professional calling was not to be his own, he turned to psychology and philosophy, completing his doctorate at Breslau in 1924. After a brief period in business, Elias took to sociology, working first as an assistant to Karl Mannheim at Frankfurt.[9] Later, he moved to the University of

Leicester. His *magnum opus* is a two-volume work, *The Civilizing Process*, the first volume of which deals with the history of manners and the second with state formation and civilization. The work was completed in 1936, published in 1939, but largely ignored until the 1960s. The reason for its neglect — the fact that it was not easily located within one discipline — is the source of its strength, for it moves effortlessly across sociology, psychology and philosophy. Its influence on educational theory, particularly in the sociology of education, has been negligible.[10] The discussion which follows, on Elias's theory, assumes no knowledge of his writings. For those who require a fuller development of particular aspects of his work, a series of references are listed in notes 9 and 10 at the end of the chapter.

The social scientific study of education is beset by the dichotomy between idealism and positivism. For example, child psychology abstracts the child from society, seeing the concept of the child as having nothing to do with history, philosophy or sociology. The child is said to 'develop' according to pre-ordained structures which are universally applicable. So, from this perspective, we can talk of *inner* desires and needs. Some strands of sociology, on the other hand, hold what Wrong has called an 'oversocialized' view of the individual.[11] That is, our identity is socialized by social forces. Given this dichotomy we end up with identity being either the totality of innate developments or the effect of social processes.

Elias's criticism has been levelled mainly at those who propounded the latter, particularly at Talcott Parsons whose conceptualization of the 'social system' he found to be both ahistorical and static (a society as 'wax museum'), with an artificial distinction between the *independent* concepts of 'ego' and 'social system'.[12] This independence was mistaken:

> I was made aware that this [i.e. his own] study brings somewhat nearer to resolution the intractable problem of the connection between individual psychological structures (so-called personality structures) and figurations formed by large numbers of interdependent individuals (social structures). It does so because it approaches both types of structures not as fixed, as usually happens, but as changing, and as interdependent aspects of the same long-term development.[13]

9

Through an historical analysis of the history of manners and courtly society since the Middle Ages, Elias postulates that what we have is a gradual evolution of self-control brought about through changes in social structure. This he calls the 'sociogenesis' of self-restraint, or 'civility', and the elegance of his analysis is that he describes the psychological and the sociological in the same terms.

During the Middle Ages, society was marked by the unbridled expression of affects and impulses. Elias terms it the warrior society. If we could have been present and had seen social life through our modern, civilized eyes, we would probably have been struck by the 'childishness' of it all. Few distinctions were made between children and adults, apart from the fact that children were simply younger. But not much turned on this age difference. Children were not to be seen as a separate social category who warranted different treatment.[14] This was because adults, like children, were not socially influenced to suppress their impulses and curb their passions. This point will now be developed.

Before about 1500, there was far less inclination to curb one's instinctual tendencies, to regulate oneself. The celebrated medieval historian Luchaire enables a readjustment of our modern perspective:

> Imagine a social state in which security for property and person did not exist: no police, and little justice, especially outside of the larger cities; each one defends his purse and his life as best he can. Robbers operate in broad day and on all roads.[15]

Elias elaborates:

> Much of what appears contradictory to us — the intensity of their piety, the violence of their fear of hell, their guilt feelings, their penitence, the immense outbursts of joy and gaiety, the sudden flaring and the uncontrollable force of their hatred and belligerence — all these, like the rapid changes of mood, are in reality symptoms of the same social and personality structure. The instincts, the emotions were vented more freely, more directly, more openly than later. *It is only to us, in whom everything is more subdued, moderate, and calculated,*

and in whom social taboos are built much more deeply into the fabric of instinctual life as self-restraints, that this unveiled intensity of piety, belligerence, or cruelty appears as contradictory [emphasis added].[16]

What Elias is describing in the behaviour of these fifteenth-century adults in their warrior society is that which we generally observe only in children, a crucial point to which we shall return.[17] Gradually, however, the history of Western *civilization* unfolds as an age when *civility*, or the self-control of affects, becomes socially required. Thereafter, so-called civilized society acted out its instincts more *vicariously* than hitherto, through spectator sports, such as viewing a boxing match, a play, or videos.

That this self-suppression of affects and impulses occurred after 1500, beginning in courtly society, has been amply documented by Elias. Table manners, the control of bodily functions, blowing one's nose and spitting all became matters of discussion in courtly circles. Elias cites in particular the treatise by Erasmus entitled *De civilitate morum puerilium* (On civility in children), published in 1530.[18] Others followed. Of most interest are those which criticize previous practices in favour of the new manners. Take Giovanni della Casa's *Galateo*, published in 1609:

> What do you think this Bishop and his noble company (*il Vescove e la sua nobile brigata*) would have said to those whom we sometimes see lying like swine with their snouts in the soup, not once lifting their heads and turning their eyes, still less their hands, from the food, puffing out both cheeks as if they were blowing a trumpet or trying to fan a fire, not eating but gorging themselves, dirtying their arms almost to the elbows and then reducing their serviettes to a state that would make a kitchen rag look clean.[19]

Other prohibitions are prescribed for bodily functions. These increasingly came to be undertaken in private, and if they were observed by another person then a sense of acute embarrassment was felt by both. The 'shame standard', as Elias terms it, changed. To develop the point further, consider the 'Brunswick Court Regulations' of 1589, reported by Elias:[20]

> One should not, like rustics who have not been to court or lived among refined and honourable people, relieve oneself without shame

11

or reserve in front of ladies, or before the doors or windows of court chambers or other rooms. Rather, everyone ought at all times and in all places to show himself reasonable, courteous, and respectful in word and gesture.

Finally, the blowing of one's nose attracted strong words of advice in Erasmus's 1530 treatise, again quoted by Elias:

> To blow your nose on your hat or clothing is rustic, and to do so with the arm or elbow befits a tradesman; nor is it much more polite to use the hand, if you immediately smear the snot on your garment.[21]

Much therefore that we would find shameful and embarrassing was commonplace before 1500. There was little sense of shame, and therefore *very little to keep from children so as to preserve their innocence*. Drawing on Elias, Postman makes the central point at issue here: *without a well-developed idea of shame, childhood cannot exist*.[22] The relatively greater threshold of shame in western Europe occurred as the feuding of the medieval period gradually gave way to a period of centralized control, epitomized by the absolute monarchy of Louis XIV in France. How this 'shame threshold' changed is now discussed.

After 1600, large domains of Europe became pacified. A feudal warrior society with decentralized political power gave way to one of absolute monarchy and a centralized state. Wherever this physical pacification occurred, 'civilizing' restraints were placed, initially, on the aristocracy's expression of affects, and subsequently on the bourgeoisie and lesser orders. Whereas hitherto the feudal lord would have used force to achieve his desires, the courtier would adopt a more manipulative, covert and scheming strategy. Later, particularly in France, the bourgeoisie incorporated these courtly elements into their notion of civilization. It was Elias's insight that this *psychological* pacification had proceeded apace with the *physical* pacification of society.[23] Under a canopy of state control, more people could go about their lives relatively free from fear of attack. City economies became more complex, the web of interconnectedness greater, the 'chains of actions' longer. Relationships between people were marked increasingly by interdependence rather than by fear and aggression. Individual impulses were curbed in favour of the common endeavour. As stated, this process was very gradual, beginning in courtly society, thence to be emulated by those of lesser status.[24] What typified this civilizing process was that the individual prevented himself from venting his desires, impulses and passions. It became shameful if he were seen to do so. Indeed, he experienced guilt even if he were *not* observed. Good manners replaced bad habits. If, in the past, he had lived in fear of attack, now he lived in fear of shame. In Elias's telling phrase, the 'battlefield had moved within'.[25]

Much of Elias's documentary evidence pertains mainly to the period from feudal society to that of absolute monarchy, particularly in France. In order to bring his approach to more recent times — that is, to a bureaucratic, market system — it is necessary for us, and Elias, to extrapolate:

> From the earliest period of the history of the Occident to the present, social functions have become more and more differentiated under the pressure of competition. The more differentiated they become, the larger grows the number of functions and thus of people on whom the individual constantly depends in all his actions. . . . The individual is compelled to regulate his conduct in an increasingly differentiated, more even and more stable manner.[26]

It is the 'interconnectedness' of modern life which requires ever-increasing self-restraint.[27] All this has relevance to childhood, and therefore to education. It is this: the central canopy of control produced a horizontal distancing between people — that is, they controlled the expression of their affects. But in addition to this horizontal distancing was a vertical one: that between child and adult.[28] As the 'civilizing process' evolves,[29] the 'childlike' behaviour of adults tends to decline. Thus, to restate the argument:

> the specific process of psychological 'growing up' in Western societies, which frequently occupies the minds of psychologists and pedagogues today, *is nothing other than the individual civilising process to which each young person, as a result of the social civilising process over many centuries, is automatically subjected from earliest childhood, to a greater or lesser degree and with greater or lesser success* [emphasis added].[30]

What the individual's transition from childhood to 'civilized' adulthood resembles is a greatly compressed version of his own

13

society's historical progression from a 'warrior society' to one wherein power was monopolized for long periods at the centre. More specifically, 'from earliest youth' the individual is trained in 'the constant restraint and foresight that he needs for adult functions'. In time, a state of 'automatic self-supervision of his drives' obtains so that his earlier impulses and drives recede from his consciousness.[31]

Elias's analysis has not been bereft of criticism. Buck-Morss regards Elias as focusing too much on an 'aristocratic zone of ballroom dancing', thereby giving an impression of society as lacking overt forms of conflict — a 'depoliticized analytic'.[32] What Elias sees as a 'gradual spreading out and trickling down of civilization from king's court to prince's court to bourgeois homes', Marxist critical theorists interpret as changes in affect which are functional for capitalism.[33] Whereas Elias emphasizes the *interdependence* of social groups, Marxists emphasize the *oppression* of classes. Drawing on Adorno, Buck-Morss defines the new personality 'traits' such as deferred gratification, self-control and asceticism as psychic prerequisites for the accumulation of capital. In other words, this new affect structure was instrumental for industrial production; the courtly regulation of affects was, so to say, an elegant affectation of the body for *aesthetic* purposes alone. Elias, however, did not claim that the mode of capitalist production was a sufficient explanation.[34] Indeed his theory of the refinement of affect behaviour since the Middle Ages should according to Sica be seen in parallel to changing modes of production.[35]

Elias also has relevance to Freudian theory. He argues that the superego is considerably, though not completely, 'sociogenetic' in origin, emerging among the bourgeoisie. For Freud, the child moves from dependence on the mother to autonomy (thereby becoming civilized). The child-as-individual, albeit one with anti-social, biological drives which need repressing, is Freud's unit of analysis. For Elias, it is individuals-in-society, in what he calls *configurations*, who should be considered. It is not that the child moves from a state of dependency on the mother, it is that he enters a general 'web' of social *inter*-dependency wherein he must regulate his affect. The notions of shame and guilt in adulthood are specific to a post-medieval period; they are not universal, biologically determined traits. To elaborate: between about 1790 and 1840 the ruling classes constantly pointed to the wantonly ribald and sensual behaviour of the poor. It was the latter whose culture was deemed to be in need of rationalization into the new moral order.

Smith, alluding to Elias, points up the intended shift required of the poor during this period: (1) their alleged volatility and lack of purpose should be replaced by stability and more certainty of purpose; (2) their gregarious sociability should give way to restricted sociability; (3) their sensuality and concrete thought patterns should be replaced by abstract thought and rationality; and (4) their (roughly) stupidity should give way to intelligence.[36] The similarity of these dimensions to modern personality and cognitive theory is striking. For example, (1) accords with Eysenck's neuroticism–stability axis; and (2) corresponds to his extroversion–introversion axis. As to (3), there is a resemblance to the concept of intelligence as measured in IQ tests. Smith concludes: 'The similarity is perhaps due to a basic continuity of assumptions, since the industrial revolution, about which psychological characteristics are deemed valuable'.[37] These affects of the poor should be repressed (at first coercively, later autonomously), not expressed. Clearly, this self-regulation would be functional for the social order of capitalism in a rationalized and systematized world, as Marxists aver; but the personality structure of the bourgeoisie and aristocracy *pre*-dates capitalism, as Elias's socio-historical analysis suggests.

All this had consequences for children. Were they to be left to express their passions and desires, or were they to suppress them in a 'civilized' manner, like their elders? These questions have been central to the education of young children ever since.

John Locke and Jean-Jacques Rousseau

The two perspectives on childhood which have emerged since the seventeenth century are best represented by John Locke's *Some Thoughts Concerning Education*, published in 1693, and Jean-Jacques Rousseau's *Emile*, published in 1762. The two approaches are debated by Rousseau:[38]

'Reason with children' was Locke's chief maxim, it is in the height of fashion at present, and I hardly think it is justified by its results; those children who have been constantly reasoned with strike me as exceedingly silly.

He goes on:

by talking to them from their earliest age in a language they do not understand you accustom them to be satisfied with words, to question all that is said to them, to think themselves as wise as their teachers . . .

But this instilling of reason was, for Rousseau, bought at the expense of compelling or manipulating the child:

Most of the moral lessons which are and can be given to children may be reduced to this formula:

Master: You must not do that.

Child: Why not?

Master: Because it is wrong.

Child: Wrong! What is wrong?

Master: What is forbidden you.

Child: Why is it wrong to do what is forbidden?

Master: You will be punished for disobedience.

Child: I will do it when no one is looking.

Master: We shall watch you.

Child: I will hide.

Master: We shall ask you what you were doing.

Child: I shall tell a lie.

Master: You must not tell lies.

Child: Why must I not tell lies?

Master: Because it is wrong, etc.

Locke's view of childhood is one which Postman has termed the 'Protestant' view whereby 'the child is an unformed person who through literacy, education, reason, *self-control and shame may be made into a civilized adult*' (my italics).[39] All this was quite the opposite to Rousseau's concern:

Our wisdom is slavish prejudice, our customs consist in *control, constraint, compulsion*. Civilised man is born and dies a slave. The infant is bound up in swaddling clothes, the corpse is nailed down in his coffin. All his life long man is *imprisoned by our institutions* [emphasis added].[40]

Rousseau, therefore, would have little to do with the emerging civilizing process as it applied to the years immediately after infancy, for it dampened the naturalness, spontaneity and joy of childhood. Rousseau did not regard childhood as an interim stage on the way to adulthood. For him, childhood was complete in itself, not adulthood 'writ small'. He thought in terms of a difference in kind, not of degree.[41] He believed that the shame and psychological pain of civility should be deferred, thereby preserving the joy and freedom of childhood. But whose definition of childhood would prevail: Locke's or Rousseau's? On balance, at the level of practice, Locke has been the more influential. The reason for this is that childhood has been structured by a set of emerging trends in industrial society, namely scientific rationality, bureaucracy, Darwinism and, initially, Protestantism. These influences are now discussed.

Science, capitalism and bureaucracy

As the age of industrial capitalism gathered pace in Europe, its dominant organizational form, bureaucracy, imposed an 'iron cage' of rationality on the populace. Weber, whose writings have provided deep insights into both the idea of bureaucracy and the 'spirit of capitalism', is clear about the efficacy of bureaucracy:

The decisive reason for the advance of bureaucratic organisation has always been its purely technical superiority over every other form. A fully developed bureaucratic apparatus stands to these other forms in much the same relation as a machine does to non-mechanical means of production. Precision, despatch, clarity, familiarity with the documents, continuity, discretion, uniformity, rigid subordination, savings in friction and in material and personal cost — all these are raised much more effectively to the optimal level by a strongly bureaucratic administration.[42]

Cold, hard, impersonal rationality prevailed. Notions of love, hatred and 'all elements of purely personal sentiment' were excluded. They were irrational and had no place in the bureaucratic scheme of things. Weber states precisely the costs of the new instrumental rationality:

> the mighty cosmos of the modern economic order . . . the iron cage [where] specialists without spirit, sensualists without heart, [are] caught in the delusion that [they] have achieved a level of development never before attained by mankind.[43]

This was the age of the specialist who depended on the competence of other specialists. It was the age of the division of labour. The Protestant ethic and what Berger *et al.* call the 'bureaucratic cognitive style' are of a piece.[44] And there is much in this 'style' which accords with what Elias might see as civilized, self-regulated behaviour, as the following elaboration of the bureaucratic cognitive style suggests.

What are its elements? First and foremost there is *orderliness*: that is, an urge to eliminate chaos by categorizing everything in taxonomies. It is 'fixating rather than innovating'.[45] Second, every aspect of life may be organized according to bureaucratic criteria. Obvious examples are timetables and spatial arrangements which fit bureaucratic patterns. And it is not only in work settings that this is seen: in the home one can find bulletin boards, lists of things to do, daily planners and intra-family 'memos'. Even when on vacation, many of us carry on as if we are contained in the bureaucracy of our work. For example, other aspects of the bureaucratic cognitive style are *predictability*, *accountability* and *efficiency*, notions which are clearly met by the car driver on vacation who assiduously measures his 'miles-per-gallon'. So embedded is the bureaucratic cognitive style that we regard it as plausible and natural. We live a life of rules, routines and rationality. Our emotions are vented privately, not publicly. Our actions must be predictable to others. We must 'stay cool'.

Our sense of fatalism is declining, as is our need to call on divine intervention. The onset of secularization has been both rapid and ironical. That is, there is an argument which states that the religion of Protestantism sowed the seeds of its own demise. Its 'ethic' is tantamount to what we used to call the 'work ethic', one which is full of maxims like 'waste not, want not', 'a place for everything and everything in its place', 'time is money', 'work now and play later'; and so on. If to these we add the Calvinist imperative that in order for an individual to become a member of God's Elect he must *accumulate*, then it is possible to understand the crucial part played by Protestantism in the furtherance of capitalism. To Protestantism's affinity with capitalism can be added the Darwinian notion of the 'survival of the fittest', an adage which gave biological and 'natural' justification to the competitive individualism of capitalism itself, and to the notion of 'individual differences' which is enshrined in psychology. But while Protestantism and Darwinism provided mutual supports for capitalism as an ideal, it was science which sustained the *technical* development of capitalism. Herein lies a clue to explain the decline of religion: science questions, explains and requires evidence; religion cannot rest on these rational means — it requires faith and blind acceptance of doctrine by its adherents.[46]

To summarize thus far: educational slogans and concepts emerge at particular historical junctures. Of concern here has been the concept of the child and how the meanings a society assigns to young children have emerged in Western Europe. In medieval times there was little distinction to be drawn between children and adults. This was not to continue beyond the Middle Ages. Beginning in courtly society, the suppression of affects marked the manifestation of civility. Power was 'wielded' increasingly in symbolic, non-physical forms among the aristocracy and bourgeoisie. 'Don't get mad, get even' emerges as a political maxim. Children of these classes had to be prepared for these forms: their affects had to be curtailed — their emotions to be *educated* along the lines suggested by Erasmus and Locke. Rousseau, however, clung to his romantic view of the young child, one which had more to do with the medieval period than with those which succeeded it. But it was not to be: capitalism, science and Darwinism all converged throughout the eighteenth and nineteenth centuries to produce a social order which became increasingly interdependent, urbanized, competitive, unequal and secular. New modes of social control, or education, were required. The fulfilment of this requirement was greatly facilitated by the rise of psychology.

Psychology, childhood and pedagogy

Psychology has had two important effects on formal education. First, through its techniques of testing it has allowed education to become concerned — some would say obsessed — with rank-ordering children. Second, theoretical frameworks derived from developmental psychology have infused pedagogical discourse with that now-familiar rhetoric of 'stages', 'growth,' 'development' and 'needs'. In what follows, a brief attempt is made to set the emergence of child psychology in an age marked by bureaucratic rationality and capitalism.

Bureaucracy provided industrial capitalism with an efficient mode of organization. Empirical science generated the theories of the material world which could be applied to manufacturing. Herbert Spencer's Darwinian maxim of 'the survival of the fittest' produced a natural, biologically based justification of the social order: that is, those who found themselves at the top of the social hierarchy could invoke scientific, objective and genetic justification of their privilege and power. To this idea of *stratification* may be added that of *classification*. If the natural world could be stratified, classified and explained according to biological considerations, then so too could the mind. A clear example of this application of empirical science to the mind is phrenology, whereby the surface features of the head allowed the phrenologist to 'read off' the characteristics of the mind 'within'. A more sophisticated development of this scientific analysis of mind was psychometry, which drew upon advances in statistics, particularly its definition of the norm and the deviation.

The convergence of the normal distribution and the naturalization of mind set the stage for the emergence of psychometry.[47] It cannot be stressed too strongly that there was a clear affinity between eugenics and psychometry. Francis Galton, a cousin of Darwin, was central to the IQ testing movement. Intelligence tests, and those which measure 'personality', regard mental states *as if* they are classifiable according to immutable, objective, natural criteria. Through testing, psychometry produced statistical norms (and deviations) against which the individual could be 'marked' and classified. This needs restating: a *statistical* norm comes to be regarded as denoting a *moral* standard (in the case of

20

a personality test). In the same way the standard deviation (a statistical term) is used to indicate immoral individuals (as defined by personality tests), whom we call deviants. Once the testing had been completed, particular 'treatments' could be proffered according to the 'individual's needs', as defined by a scientific methodology which produced 'hard data'.

The classic example of how the spurious assumptions of psychometry *produced* social categories was the IQ test. In 1906, the National Association of Manufacturers in the USA required three kinds of employees: the abstract thinkers who could fill managerial positions; the concrete thinkers for the production line; and those with more general abilities who could comprise the increasing clerical class. Mass IQ testing *produced* these three pre-defined clusters which have formed the basis of school-based streaming ever since. The fact that it was the working-class children who swelled the ranks of 'concrete thinkers' was conveniently glossed over, as was any critical analysis of what had counted as 'intelligence'.[48] Therefore, what initially purported to be a scientific and ideologically neutral endeavour turned out to constitute a procedure of social regulation. The influence of psychometry on early education will be alluded to in later chapters.

The science of pedagogy

Eighteenth-century philosophers rejected the notion that the mind is pre-given, an innately constructed entity. On the contrary, the mind could be formed through education, given a scientific pedagogy. John Locke's *Essay Concerning Human Understanding* had earlier set the stage for the rejection of the theory of innate ideas and instincts by his materialist theory that, at birth, the mind was a *tabula rasa* awaiting the influence of education. The expression of impulses, emotions and instincts could be superseded by man's rational development through education. But how did learning take place? Central to the theoretical analysis of the mind was Hartley's *Observations on Man*, published in 1749. Hartley argued that the individual apprehended knowledge of the external world through the senses. These sensations were then subjected to physiological processes in the nervous system whereby they were associated into particular coherent structures

21

in the mind — hence his theory of 'associationism'. Thus, in order to educate a child using Hartley's theory, it would be necessary to structure his experiences so that they would be easily associated. It is pertinent to note here that the idea of education — of *forming habits* — accords with Elias's observation that post-medieval society limited the expression of affects in favour of self-control. Education would offer the means to this end and it would be based on the insights of psychology.

At this point it is important to restate Rousseau's relevance to Hartley's *scientific* theory of pedagogy. Both men set much store on *experience* as a learning medium, but Rousseau emphasized the 'naturalness' of the child — his play, joy and freedom. The concerns of both men were expressed in Robert Owen's Institution for the Formation of Character at New Lanark, Scotland, in 1816, for it was there that both discussion and affection were stressed. The children were to be happy, not punished.[49] True, it was an institution — and would therefore not have been to Rousseau's liking — but it was, by all accounts, a pleasant one, and it did not exclude the children of the poor. New Lanark, however, was not the common educational experience of the working-class child. Later, the monitorial system combined efficiency and compliance through a pedagogy of continuous, *overt* surveillance and regulation. In its wake came the school class as the unit of *instruction* rather than regulation. Thus it was that the bureaucratic concerns of punctuality, obedience, deference and impersonality were, initially, overtly taught in schools. Later, after they had become part of common expectation, these 'traits' were 'taught' through the hidden curriculum.[50] (This could be contrasted with Froebel's pedagogy, which found its expression in the more mannered circles of bourgeois European society.) But it must be stressed that the Industrial Revolution caused the children of the poor to suffer greatly. Beaten, starved and tired, they exhibited a 'morality' not at one with the civility of their 'betters'. Consider, for example, the testimony of Matthew Crabtree to the Select Committee on the Regulation of the Labour of Children in Mills and Factories of the United Kingdom:[51]

> Can you speak as to the effect of this labour in the mills and factories on the morals of the children, as far as you have observed? As far

as I have observed with regard to morals in the mills, there is everything
about them that is disgusting to every one conscious of correct
morality.

Do you find that the children, the females especially, are very early
demoralized in them? — They are. Is their language indecent? —
Very indecent; and both sexes take great familiarities with each other
in the mills, *without at all being ashamed of their conduct* [emphasis added].

What is fascinating about the Victorian attitude to children is
this: children were treated sadistically, yet they were idealized in
Victorian culture: 'Children became the last symbols of purity in
a world which was seen as increasingly ugly.'[52] Not all Victorian
writers idealized the purity of children — Dickens is an obvious
exception — but many did, none more so than Lewis Carroll. It
was he who kept alive the pre-verbal fantasies of children, thereby
implicitly questioning the Victorian 'morality' of repressing the
child. Lewis Carroll had probably struck a raw nerve: such was
the guilt which Victorians felt over their sadism and desires that
they responded by creating characters who had no guilt and no
questionable desires at all.[53]

After 1900, children became increasingly the object of scientific
study. The theoretical frameworks which were generated drew
upon aspects of the wider social structure. The influence of
Darwinian theory and statistics has already been referred to in
connection with psychometry. Now the relationship between social
structure and behaviourist psychology is considered. Implicit in
behaviourism is that the child is infinitely malleable in the face
of his environment. This clearly echoes Locke's *tabula rasa* position.
It sets aside, therefore, considerations of an inner nature: it would
be redundant to talk about 'back to basics' because there are
no basics. Also implied in behaviourism is the importance of
the observable, empirical response to a stimulus. Thus inner
mental states can be read off from the behaviour which 'reveals'
them. The influence of behaviourism on child-rearing was considerable and is very much associated with Watson's *Psychological
Care of Infant and Child*, published in 1928.

The association between behaviourism and bureaucratic rationality is obvious. Indeed, it could be argued that it calls for the
bureaucratization of child-rearing just as F.W. Taylor bureau-
cratized the assembly line according to the tenets of scientific

management theory. (Taylorism takes its name from F.W. Taylor, an engineer turned management consultant, whose work *The Principles of Scientific Management*, published in 1911, became the guiding force behind Henry Ford's philosophy of management at his Detroit car factory. He advocated that the production process be reduced to its smallest component tasks, the completion of which should be monitored minutely in order to maximize efficiency and profit — hence the time-and-motion studies. During the 1920s, Taylorism was applied to schooling in the USA. For a discussion, see R. E. Callahan's *Education and the Cult of Efficiency*.) Behaviourist child-rearing had no regard for sentimentality, love and cuddles. Feeding on demand gave way to feeding on time; the child had to curb the desire to be fed just as the mother had to repress her desire to feed; caring gave way to training; the child was monitored and managed, bearing the brunt of this cult of efficiency. The increasing self-regulation and suppression of affects discussed by Elias therefore take on a particular poignancy in the case of behaviourism.

Other schools of psychology looked *beneath*, not at, surface behaviour, none more so than that of the developmental psychology of Jean Piaget, whose influence on British primary education can be detected in both the Hadow Reports of the 1930s and the Plowden Report of 1967. Piaget (1896–1980) was a prolific writer, the author of over forty books. His theory of *genetic* epistemology (my emphasis) takes us away from the limitless possibilities of behaviourism back to a 'basic'. The basic is that children progress *naturally* from a state of emotionality to one of scientific rationality, stage by stage, given the correct environment of experience. While this progression, or 'development', was said to be linear, its pace could vary — it was spontaneous. The spontaneity could best be effected through play (as had been advocated by Froebel and Rousseau), and would have the added benefit of having a cathartic effect. This catharsis would serve to release aggression as 'child's play' rather than as future adult violence. What links developmental psychology to the Taylorist approach to factory management is the necessity for *monitoring*: that is, Taylor's time-and-motion studies accord with the continual monitoring advocated by developmental psychology in order to ascertain what stage the child is at, and whether or not the child is ready for the next one.

There is a coincidence, albeit a superficial one, between Elias and Piaget. Piaget is a structuralist: that is, he seeks universal principles of thought formation that are valid for all human minds at all times.[54] Unlike Elias, Piaget's analysis is not grounded in history. What is striking is that the individual's development from a state of emotionality to one of scientific rationality (Piaget) accords with the social construction of childhood from medieval to modern times: that is, from the free expression of affects in the Middle Ages to the self-regulated, rational behaviour of today (Elias). In a similar vein, consider Froebel's assertion that: 'In the development of the inner life of the individual man the history of the spiritual development of the race is repeated'.[55] Had Piaget been able to observe 'childhood' in the Middle Ages he would not have observed children 'develop'. All this raises the question posed by Venn and Walkerdine: was Piagetian developmental psychology actually instrumental in *producing* children who develop through Piaget's stages?[56] (With some acidity, Bronfenbrenner has stated that 'much of developmental psychology, as it now exists, is the science of the strange behaviour of children in strange situations with strange adults for the briefest possible periods of time.'[57]) Spiecker provides a useful illustration of this:

> The mother treats the young child from birth as if he were already a person with needs, wishes and intentions; the child is, to use Buber's words, approached as 'Thou', not as 'It'. *The interactions between mother and baby are determined to a large degree by the conceptual framework within which the mother approaches her child; it is this framework which needs further research.* [emphasis added] . . . The infant develops in a *human* manner because the mother initiates him into a pattern of joint action within a field of meanings. Because he is spoken to *as if* he were already a person, the child, in his relationship with those significant other(s), *becomes* a developing person [emphasis in original].[58]

What these authors are stressing is that the end-stage of Piaget's development (scientific rationality) is not a *naturally* required outcome, but one functional for a highly differentiated, techno-bureaucratic society.[59] Moreover, child-centred pedagogy entails constant *monitoring* of the child's 'development'. Children exposed to this 'invisible' pedagogy will apparently regulate *their own* movements and social relationships.[60] This concept of 'invisible' pedagogy is now discussed.

Visible and invisible pedagogy

The relationship between social structure, school organization and individual identity has been little discussed in nursery education. An exception is Bernstein's *Class and Pedagogies: Visible and Invisible*.[61] The paper is part of a collection[62] which analyses the relationship between the class structure (at the macro level), the forms of pedagogy and assessment (at school organization level), and the identity of the child (individual level).[63] The central argument is as follows. Drawing upon Durkheim, Bernstein asserts that 'every industrialised society produces organic solidarity', by which he means a society marked by a complex interdependency of roles.[64] Unlike Durkheim, however, he sees two forms of organic solidarity which 'arise out of developments of the division of labour within class societies'.[65] These developments include a shift from the production of goods to the provision of services, and a change from hierarchical control to greater self-control. Following Durkheim, the first form of organic solidarity is *individualized*, and it associates with what he refers to as the 'old' middle class, whose status and power are based more on physical than on 'symbolic property'. Members of this class will have been socialized more 'visibly': that is, they will tend to arrange objects in fixed, neat configurations, and they will see their identities and roles as similarly inflexible. Ambiguity and discretion will be minimized. On the other hand, the 'new' middle class, who are loosely defined as the new agents of symbolic control, e.g. those who are filling the ever expanding major and minor professional class, concerned with the servicing of persons,[66] will express *personalized* organic solidarity. This 'new' fraction of the middle class who control symbolic property will be socialized more 'invisibly'. Applied to the pre- and infant school, the invisible pedagogy is one whereby control will be achieved implicitly: that is, the child may rearrange and personalize the context which has been pre-defined by the teacher; the child will have the apparent discretion as to what, when, with whom and how he acts within this pre-set arrangement; and the criteria for evaluating or assessing the child will be 'multiple and diffuse'.[67] It is possible here to suggest a parallel between the hierarchical control within Weber's ideal typical bureaucracy and the 'visible' pedagogy, and an attendant parallel between human relations management and the 'invisible pedagogy's' implicit form of control.

But this presumed mode of socialization within the 'new' middle class poses a dilemma for the mother: that is, in order to accomplish effectively this 'invisible' control she must be with the child for a great deal of the time, but, by so doing, she has to suppress her own occupational ambition and identity. The tensions arising from this dilemma may be partly resolved if she is able to entrust her child to a nursery school whose pedagogy mirrors her own. There is, therefore, an implied causal relationship between mother and school:

> Thus the middle class mother in a context of personalised organic solidarity provides the model for the pre-school infant school teacher.[68]

To repeat, for Bernstein there is a causal relationship between changes in the class structure, the primary socialization pattern of the new middle-class home, and the invisible pedagogy of the pre-school:

> In the microcosm of the nursery or infant class, we can see embryonically the new form of transmission of class relationships.

Bernstein's thesis has been criticized theoretically and empirically. Sharp, a Marxist, has argued that Bernstein offers what amounts to a structural functionalist perspective which leaves unexplained the technological changes which are at the root of his thesis: that is, Bernstein has not sought to explain the introduction of new technology and organizational forms.[69] For Sharp, they can be regarded as capitalism's quest for efficiency and profit. Moreover, Bernstein equates class with occupation and income, a definition which fails to discuss class *relationships* in their economic, ideological and political aspects.[70] King, taking a Weberian standpoint, criticizes Bernstein's view that schools will adapt to the wider economic structure, thereby leaving out of the account the possibility that those in schools will offer varying interpretations of that structure, and will act accordingly.[71] All this is quite apart from findings that the invisible pedagogy is little in evidence in the infant school, even middle-class ones.[72]

Other evidence drawn from nursery schools is inconclusive. Kanter has coined the term 'organization child' as typifying the 'professional' children (of parents who are professionals) in the nursery school observed by her in the American Midwest in 1965.[73] In a more recent American study, Lubeck undertook participant observation in two nursery schools: one, a black working-class Head Start nursery,[74] the other, a middle-class white nursery. Her analysis offers some support for Bernstein's 'invisible' pedagogy in the 'new' middle-class nursery, but not in the Head Start centre.[75] Unfortunately, Lubeck does not relate her findings to Bernstein's 'pedagogies' paper, though she does cite his earlier sociolinguistic work.

Like Elias, Bernstein draws on Durkheim. Moreover, his concept of the 'invisible' pedagogy accords with Elias's analysis that modes of control in highly differentiated societies will become increasingly based on self-regulation rather than on hierarchical authority. Bernstein, however, purports to explain the shift from 'visible' to 'invisible' control solely on the basis of technological and occupational change in capitalism. Elias would doubtless regard this as too narrow a theory to posit. His more informed historical perspective, which *pre-dates* these changes in economic production, shows that the shift to greater self-regulation had already been set in train. While these economic considerations to which Bernstein alludes are a necessary part of the explanation, they are not a sufficient one. The importance of both theorists, however, is that they move our explanation of individual identities in early educational settings away from the restricted psychological perspective which has hitherto prevailed.

Finally, a word about the society at issue here: Scotland.[76] An education system — its organization, curriculum, pedagogy, mode of assessment — is itself a cultural creation whose character is the product of its history, a history with political, economic and cultural patterns. Scottish infant education has been referred to as being more formal than that in England.[77] This assertion is not supported by research, not because the assertion is untrue, but because comparative study has not yet been undertaken. A very cursory analysis of the history of Scottish culture, however, can suggest that the cultural conditions for didactic, as opposed to child-centred, pedagogy are rooted in its history.[78]

Central to the analysis is Calvinism. 'In explaining Scottish character nothing is more important than religion'.[79] The political effects of the Church in Scotland were considerable, for it was the Church which stood out against a nobility which was bent on allegiance to the English crown. The people looked to the Church as the saviour of their souls from the Devil and their society from the English. The Church, however, directed its energies more towards saving souls from damnation than to repelling the English. Throughout the eighteenth century it stood as the cultural arbiter of Scotland. Science had no place in a land of sermons. Whereas, in England, a more secular climate admitted a science based on inductive reasoning, in Scotland theological thought prevailed, permitting only deductive reasoning. Dogma prevented debate, leaving only quiescence.[80] When entrepreneurial capitalism entered Scotland it found a society whose populace had been pacified by ecclesiastical domination. It found a people whose inclination was to accept hierarchy, to know its place, and to be fearful of God. Capitalism, directed from England, heralded the increasing economic and political domination of Scotland. Control, hitherto exerted by the Church, was now in the hands of the English, and a new culture of dependency emerged. A cultural invasion, to use Freire's concept, had been made, and had to be sustained.[81] The new pedagogy of the oppressed had all the hallmarks of didacticism. It was of a piece with the earlier ecclesiastical didacticism on which it was superimposed. Scotland was receptive to and sustained a visible didactic pedagogy. The extent to which this cultural tide now flows is a matter for empirical research. What can be said is that, between 1965 and 1988, official thinking behind infant education emanating from the Scottish Education Department had rejected traditional, didactic pedagogy in favour of child-centredness, but recent policy suggests a strong move away from progressivism towards the more formal, didactic Scottish tradition.[82] In any case, there have been indications that teachers in most schools are still more at one with the tradition of didacticism than with the tenets of progressive education.[83] Policies are ideals. If a culture cannot receive them, they will not be implemented.

SUMMARY

The purpose of this chapter has been twofold: to consider from an historical standpoint what counts as childhood; to offer a sociological explanation of these definitions of childhood, drawing on the sociology of Elias. This enables a shift from a psychological perspective on the child to one which regards what appear to be psychological 'traits' in children as partly 'sociogenetic' in origin. The interplay of romanticism, the state, scientific rationality, Darwinism and capitalism all produced consequences for childhood and pedagogy which are still with us. They can be observed to differing degrees in that institution which an increasing number of young children attend, namely the nursery school. The study which follows is not meant to be an exhaustive test of Elias's analysis. I have used his theory to suggest a way of interpreting early childhood education which moves theory away from its current stress on psychology. The nurseries which are discussed hereafter generated ethnographic data which may be related to, and perhaps be explained by, macrosociological theory.

NOTES AND REFERENCES

1. Bernstein, B. 'Class and pedagogies: visible and invisible' (1975). In Bernstein, B. *Class, Codes and Control*, Volume III. 2nd edition. London: Routledge & Kegan Paul, 1977.
2. Squibb, P. G. 'The concept of intelligence — a sociological perspective'. *Sociological Review*, **21**, 57–75, 1973.
3. Postman, N. *The Disappearance of Childhood*. London: W. H. Allen, 1982.
4. Pollock, L. *Forgotten Children: Parent–Child Relations from 1500 to 1900*. Cambridge: Cambridge University Press, 1983; and James, A. and Prout, A. *Constructing and Reconstructing Childhood: Contemporary Issues in the Sociological Study of Childhood*. Lewes: Falmer Press, 1990.
5. Postman, op. cit. (3), pp. 120–42.
6. Opie, I. and Opie, P. *The Lore and Language of Schoolchildren*. London: Oxford University Press, 1959.
7. Meyrowitz, J. 'The adultlike child and the childlike adult: socialization in an electronic age'. *Daedalus*, **113**, 19–48, 1984.
8. Ibid., p. 46.
9. For a full discussion of Elias's biography, see Aya, R. 'Norbert Elias and the civilizing process'. *Theory and Society*, **5** (2), 219–28, 1978.
10. Eve has compared his work to that of Bowles and Gintis, and of Bourdieu and Passeron: see Eve, M. 'What is the social? On the

methodological work of Norbert Elias'. *Quaderni di Sociologia*, **30** (1), 22–48, 1980. See also Smith, J.V. 'Manners, morals, and mentalities: reflections on the popular enlightenment of early nineteenth century Scotland'. In Humes, W. and Paterson, H.M. (eds) *Scottish Culture and Scottish Education*. Edinburgh: John Donald, 1983; and Bantock, G.H. 'Educating the emotions: a historical perspective'. Paper presented to the Standing Conference on Studies in Education. London: King's College London, 1985.

11. Wrong, D. 'The over-socialized conception of man in modern sociology'. *American Sociological Review*, **26**, 183–93, 1961.

12. Elias, N. *The Civilizing Process*. Volume 1, *The History of Manners*, translated by E. Jeffcott. Oxford: Basil Blackwell, 1978, p. 228. (Originally published in 1939 by Haus zum Falken, Basel.)

13. Ibid., p. 225.

14. Tuchman, B.W. *A Distant Mirror*. New York: Knopf, 1978, p. 50.

15. Luchaire, A. *Social Justice at the Time of Philip Augustus*. New York: Holt, 1912, p. 8.

16. Elias, op. cit. (12), p. 200.

17. Robinson has questioned Elias's account of warrior society in the Middle Ages: see Robinson, R.J. '*The Civilizing Process*: some remarks on Elias's social history'. *Sociology*, **21**, 1–17, 1987.

18. See also Bantock, op. cit. (10).

19. Transcribed in Elias, op. cit. (12), p. 90.

20. Ibid., p. 131.

21. Ibid., p. 144.

22. Postman, op. cit. (3), p. 9.

23. Aya, R. 'Norbert Elias and the civilizing process'. *Theory and Society*, **5** (2), 222, 1978.

24. Elias, N. *The Civilizing Process*. Volume 2, *State Formation and Civilization*, translated by E. Jeffcott. Oxford: Basil Blackwell, 1982, pp. 250–1. (Originally published in 1939 by Haus zum Falken, Basel.)

25. Ibid., p. 242.

26. Ibid., p. 232.

27. There is an unacknowledged intellectual debt to Durkheim here; see Sica, A. 'Sociogenesis versus psychogenesis: the unique sociology of Norbert Elias'. *Mid-American Review of Sociology*, **9** (1), 49–78, 1984.

28. Buck-Morss, S. Review of Elias's *The Civilising Process*, Volume 1, op. cit. (12). *Telos*, **37**, 185, 1978.

29. The term 'evolve' here is not meant to imply a teleological analysis. It is important to stress that this 'web' of connectedness is *not* 'rational' or, for that matter, 'irrational', for it 'is set in motion *blindly* [my italics], and kept in motion by the autonomous dynamics of a web of relationships . . .' (Elias, op. cit. (24), 232).

30. Elias, op. cit. (12), p. xiii.

31. Elias, op. cit. (24), p. 241.
32. Buck-Morss, op. cit. (28).
33. Ibid., p. 188.
34. Elias, op. cit. (24), p. 235.
35. Sica, op. cit. (27), pp. 42, 71, 1984. For an analysis of Elias's theory of state formation, see Van Benthem van den Bergh, G. 'The interconnection between processes of state and class formation'. *Acta Politica*, **11** (3), 289–311, 1976. For a defence of Elias against critical theory, see Kuzmics, H. 'Elias's theory of civilization'. *Telos*, **61**, 83–99, 1984.
36. Smith, J.V. 'Manners, morals, and mentalities: reflections on the popular enlightenment of early nineteenth century Scotland'. In Humes, W. and Paterson, H.M. (eds) *Scottish Culture and Scottish Education*. Edinburgh: John Donald, 1983, p. 47.
37. Ibid., p. 54.
38. Rousseau, J.-J. *Emile*, translated by B. Foxley. London: J.M. Dent, 1974, p. 54. First published 1762.
39. Postman, op. cit. (3), p. 59.
40. Rousseau, op. cit. (38), p. 10.
41. Entwistle, H. *Child-Centred Education*. London: Methuen, 1970, p. 78.
42. Weber, M. *Economy and Society*, Vols 1 and 2. Berkeley: University of California Press, 1978, p. 350. Originally published in 1922.
43. Ibid., p. 182.
44. Berger, P., Berger, B. and Kellner, H. *The Homeless Mind*. Harmondsworth: Penguin, 1973.
45. Ibid., p. 49.
46. But for a dissenting view see Douglas, M. 'The effects of modernization on religious change'. *Daedalus*, **111**, 1–19, 1982.
47. Venn, C. 'The subject of psychology'. In Henriques, J., Holloway, W., Urwin, C., Venn, C. and Walkerdine, V. (eds) *Changing the Subject: Psychology, Social Regulation and Subjectivity*. London: Methuen, 1984, p. 141.
48. Nasaw, D. *Schooled to Order*. New York: Oxford University Press, 1979.
49. It has also been argued that Owen's purposes centred on profit and that New Lanark represented the forerunner of 'human relations' management theory. For a discussion, see Hamilton, D. 'Robert Owen and education: a reassessment'. In Humes and Paterson, op. cit. (36).
50. Vallance, E. 'Hiding the hidden curriculum'. *Curriculum Inquiry*, **38**, 5–21, 1973.
51. Original 1832, quoted in Sommerville, C.J. *The Rise and Fall of Childhood*. London: Sage, 1982, p. 164.
52. Sommerville, op. cit. (51), p. 168.
53. Ibid., p. 172.
54. See Gibson, R. *Structuralism and Education*. London: Hodder & Stoughton, especially Chapter 3.

55. Froebel, F., quoted in Rusk, R. and Scotland, J. *Doctrines of the Great Educators*. London: Macmillan, 1979.

56. Venn, C., op. cit. (47); Walkerdine, V. 'Developmental psychology and the child-centred pedagogy: the insertion of Piaget into early education'. In Henriques *et al.* op. cit. (47).

57. Quoted in Ingleby, D. 'Development in social context'. In Richards, M. and Light, P. (eds) *Children of Social Worlds: Development in a Social Context*. London: Polity Press, 1986, p. 303.

58. Spiecker, B. 'The pedagogical relationship'. *Oxford Review of Education*, **10** (2), p. 207, 1984.

59. In a similar vein, recent discussions on 'learning strategies' also show a strong affinity with the terminology of techno-bureaucratic concepts. Nisbet and Shucksmith have constructed a 'list of commonly mentioned strategies': (a) asking questions; (b) planning; (c) monitoring; (d) checking; (e) revising; (f) self-testing: see Nisbet, J. and Shucksmith, J. *Learning Strategies*. London: Routledge & Kegan Paul, 1986, p. 28.

60. Bernstein, 1975, op. cit. (1).

61. Ibid.

62. Bernstein, 1977, op. cit. (1).

63. See also Bernstein, B. 'On pedagogic discourse'. In Richardson, J.G. (ed.) *Handbook of Theory and Research for the Sociology of Education*. New York: Greenwood Press, 1986.

64. Bernstein, B., 1975, op. cit. (1), p. 26.

65. Ibid.

66. Ibid.

67. Ibid., p. 23.

68. Ibid., p. 28.

69. Sharp, R. *Knowledge, Ideology and the Politics of Schooling: Towards a Marxist Analysis of Schooling*. London: Routledge & Kegan Paul, 1980.

70. Ibid., p. 55.

71. King, R. 'In search of the invisible pedagogy'. *Sociology*, **13**, 445–58, 1979.

72. Hartley, D. 'Some consequences of teachers' definitions of boys and girls in two infant schools'. Exeter: Unpublished PhD thesis, University of Exeter, 1977; and Hartley, D. *Understanding the Primary School*. London: Croom Helm, 1985; and King, R. *All Things Bright and Beautiful?* London: Wiley, 1978.

73. Kanter, R. 'The organisation child: experience management in a nursery school'. *Sociology of Education*, **45** (2), 186–212, 1972.

74. Head Start was a compensatory education programme initiated during President Johnson's term of office.

75. Lubeck, S. *Sandbox Society: Early Education in Black and White America — A Comparative Ethnography*. London: Falmer Press, 1985, p. 138.

76. The education system in Scotland (apart from university education)

is administered by the Scottish Office Education Department, and not by the Department of Education and Science in London.

77. Roberts, A.F.B. 'Scotland and infant education in the nineteenth century'. *Scottish Educational Studies*, 4 (1), 39–45, 1972.

78. I rely here heavily on Farquharson, E. 'Culture and pedagogy: a socio-historical analysis of the "Primary Memorandum" in Scotland (1965)'. University of Dundee: Unpublished PhD thesis, 1990.

79. Notestein, W. *The Scot in History: A Study of the Interplay of Character and History*. London: Cape, 1946, p. 150.

80. Buckle, H.T. *On Scotland and the Scotch Intellect*. Chicago: University of Chicago Press, 1970. First published 1857.

81. Freire, P. *The Politics of Education, Culture, Power and Liberation*. Basingstoke: Macmillan, 1985.

82. Scottish Education Department. *Curriculum and Assessment in Scotland: A Policy for the '90s*. Edinburgh: SED, 1987; and Hartley, D. and Roger, A. *Curriculum and Assessment in Scotland: A Policy for the '90s*. Edinburgh: Scottish Academic Press, 1990.

83. Scottish Education Department. *Teaching and Learning in Primary 4 and Primary 7*. Edinburgh: HMSO, 1980.

CHAPTER 3

Inside the Nursery School

'Research methodologies in social science are themselves elements of culture'.[1] In a society marked by scientific rationality, the quest for objectivity in the social world follows in the wake of the scientific method of the 'hard', natural sciences. The discussion of intelligence testing in the previous chapter is an example. Data derived from research in the social sciences will command greater appeal if they manifest 'robustness', not 'softness'. When I began to undertake school-based research in the early 1970s, I was caught between the previous concern with 'number-crunching' and a more intuitive, empathetic methodology which drew on Weberian sociology. My research on the relationship between gender and social class in two infant schools straddled the quantitative–qualitative divide.[2] In retrospect, the use of the quantitative method in classroom settings in that study may have been over-done, but I was mindful of the importance then of classroom interaction analyses.[3] They were of importance in educational research for a number of reasons: first, because they superimposed a statistical (and therefore scientific) gloss on the activities of teachers and children; and second, their comparative nature avoided the charge of non-generalizability. What I now realize is that this methodology — with its fragmentation of classroom life, with its checklists and time-sampling, and with its emphasis on the surface features of school life — was very much a reflection of the 'bureaucratic cognitive style' which Berger *et al.* have described.[4] There remains, nevertheless, the difficulty which those involved in a more qualitative approach face: that is, the fine-grained, 'soft' accounts of classroom life which they produce may be *anthropologically* fascinating, in the sense that they let us see another 'world', but *theoretically* they are lacking in that they do not explain these fine-grained descriptions. In this sense, therefore, they constitute an empiricism whereby the ethnographic data must merely speak for themselves. The readers of a work

35

such as this may come to it with different expectations: first are those whose interests relate more to the feel of life in early education (perhaps those working in initial early education programmes); others may wish to consider the explanatory power of the sociological analysis and thence compare it with other similar studies. In sociological jargon, the former may expect more of the 'micro' data; the latter may seek the 'macro'-sociological explanation of the data themselves.

Any piece of research is guided by a conceptual framework: a way of deciding what to look at, how to look at it, and how to make sense of what has been looked at. I shall now address the elements of this conceptual framework in turn. The sociological study of nursery and infant schools is not well developed, especially in respect of nursery schools. In research that has focused on the infant school, the emphasis has been on an anthropological approach, perhaps exemplified by Rist's longitudinal study of an American urban kindergarten and his later study of the effects of 'bussing' black children to a white, middle-class elementary school.[5] Other American studies include those by Kanter and Lubeck, the latter being in the ethnographic tradition.[6] In England, Hartley and King adopted symbolic interactionist and Weberian perspectives respectively in their studies of urban infant schools.[7] The work of Pollard also furthers the ethnographic study of English infant schools,[8] though he has recently called for a methodology which combines both quantitative and qualitative methods in a complementary fashion, an approach which I adopted in my study of a Scottish multi-ethnic primary school.[9] Studies by Armstrong, Anyon, the Berlaks and Nias are also relevant.[10]

My interest in the sociology of nursery education arose out of both professional and personal concerns. I had been aware of Bernstein's important paper on 'visible' and 'invisible' pedagogies and the relative lack of empirical support for the 'invisible' pedagogy which he speculated would emerge in infant education.[11] All of these studies had been undertaken in primary schools, not nursery schools, and I was curious to take the sociological analysis 'down' to nursery schools, particularly as one of my own children was attending one. However, I wished to ground the study theoretically and thereby go beyond an overly descriptive account.

The ethnographer is concerned with what people take for granted — what they regard as natural. Those who share a common occupation may produce a culture, a shared way of seeing, which is sustained by rituals, routines and rules, most of which are followed habitually, without reflection. This is not to say that all who share a common institutional setting are at one in their views, even when an outsider might be given to think that a common culture exists. Thus, a headteacher may declare his or her school to be a 'happy family', but a certain degree of 'feuding' may gradually reveal itself to an observer. To the outsider, the 'shop-talk' and other distinguishing symbols have to be defined and explained, and this requires a sustained presence among the 'actors' by the observer.

This leads to the question, 'How can the outside observer understand those whom he or she observes?' Schutz is helpful here.[12] He distinguishes between two types of understanding. The first he terms 'observational' understanding: that is, the observer apprehends an event through his or her senses. So, for example, if I observe six children sitting on a mat in a nursery school, then I will have achieved observational understanding. That is, I will have apprehended that event through my senses and would be in a position to describe it to someone else. Some classroom observers who undertake 'interaction analysis' bring to a classroom an observational grid which they use to describe life in classrooms. The grid comprises a pre-specified set of categories, and whenever an observed event fits a category it is checked off. In this way the observer produces a categorized description which is reducible to statistics, each statistic representing a discrete event. None of this, however, tells us why these events occurred, or how they were related to each other. In short, these accounts are bereft of a second type of understanding, or what Schutz calls 'motivational understanding'.

Let us return to the children sitting on the mat. In order for the observers to achieve motivational understanding of that observation they need to impute the meanings which those children intended before they sat on the mat. In other words, there is a need to ask *why* they did it, not just *what* they did. But if we are simply detached, non-participant observers we are not in a position to ask them. (The reason why we choose to be non-participant observers is because we do not wish to disturb and distort the situation which we wish to observe. Nevertheless, some disturbance is likely to occur, particularly at first, but may be perceived as minimal later.[13]) Indeed, even if we were to ask the children, they might find the question superfluous, if not silly. This is because most of them, like us, act in a semi-aware, habitual, unreflecting manner. Our lives are routine, even dull. Rarely do we pause to ask why things are the way they are. We forget that reality is a social construction which may be reconstructed in other ways, although there are costs in doing so.[14] If, however, we continually questioned why we intended to do this, not that, then we would quickly become exhausted. That is why, perhaps, being with young children is so tiring: they have yet to make sense of the world in a consistent way. Their habits are not formed. They always want to know *why*.

To return to the non-participant observer, the sitting-on-the-mat event may be explained historically. That is, if on previous occasions the teacher later came and read a story to the children who were sitting on the mat then the observer may impute the meaning which explains the children's actions. The key requirement, therefore, is empathy, or *Verstehen*, as Weber termed it. Over a period of time the outsider, in this case the observer, is able to combine events into patterns of repeated actions. Trends emerge. What hitherto had seemed haphazard and strange is now rendered orderly and natural. Once this stage has been reached, the observer is in danger of 'going native': he or she is unable to maintain the detached position, the anthropological strangeness, required to produce an impartial, dispassionate account.

This raises the question of the degree of disinterest which is achievable by the observer at the *beginning* of a study. To say that observers can suspend their everyday way of seeing when embarking on a study seems impossible.[15] At best, it seems possible only to be aware of, and to state clearly, what their preconceptions are. This is what Weber meant by 'value-freedom' in research: it is not that researchers are entirely bereft of values, but that they make explicit what they are. In this study, my conceptual framework for interpreting life in nursery schools was informed by Berger *et al.*'s concept of the 'bureaucratic cognitive style', and by Elias's argument that the 'civilizing process' requires increasing thresholds of shame and self-control. To these have been added the further insight by Elias that forms of affect control vary according to social status.

On entering the first nursery school as a researcher rather than a parent I was struck by a fact which set it apart from the infant schools which I had studied. It was that everything and everyone was visible. It was open-plan. This proved to be a mixed blessing: on the one hand the staff were used to being 'on view' to each other, and I was merely an additional body to see and be seen; on the other hand, it made it very difficult to overhear staff and children. In respect of the latter consideration, I thought about using either radio-microphones or video cameras, but as there was no research funding for the study the use of this expensive technology would have required me to seek money at the very moment I was ready to pursue the research. I suspected, too, that microphones and cameras would prove to be too intrusive. I was very aware that nursery schools were uncharted waters for sociological research, and I tried to be as sensitive as I could to the staff's concerns. In particular, I informed the staff of each school that if, for whatever reason, my presence was either temporarily or permanently not desired, then I would willingly take my leave.

I took the role of non-participant observer. That said, I conversed with children and staff whenever approached — to have done otherwise would have been discourteous. My note-taking was done openly. I took pains not to be seen talking too much to any one particular person or group. At one school, however, I was informed that the headteacher had been asking some staff what I had been talking to them about. This raises the sensitive matter of the political effects of a research endeavour of this kind. A researcher produces a report which may unintentionally serve as an 'aid' to management. In other words, the reported data may have consequences for institutional members' careers, particularly if their status is low and provided that they can be identified accurately by officialdom. There is also the matter of the response to the findings by those who helped to generate them, namely the staff and children. If a full-draft report is given to staff they may focus only on the parts which they think pertain to them as individuals. This would be in contrast to the general, not particular, focus of the researcher, who has had access to a greater range of events and people.[16] Furthermore, this open access to a draft may lead to attempts to negotiate away what are perceived to be unfavourable data and analysis, a matter which would be tantamount to tampering with, if not managing, the research. On the other hand, to take one's data and leave would be a discourtesy to those whose forbearance and cooperation had hitherto been freely given. Gone, too, would be the opportunity to test the researcher's overall analysis against the reactions of the participants themselves. Ethnography can render explicit what the teacher implicitly and habitually says and does. The effects of this are difficult to predict, for to see ourselves as others see us may not be easy. It can be uncomfortable, even threatening, particularly if one appears to be different from one's peers. These reactions a researcher cannot anticipate. For the teacher who is prepared to discuss the research data, there is the possibility that he or she may see anew his or her professional practice. And this consideration of the teacher's practice can provide the basis for a deeper analysis. In other words, ethnography can generate an initial discussion of the *means of teaching* as the basis for a fuller analysis of the ends of education itself. Hence I decided to send a full draft to each of the nursery schools/units, and to invite reactions.

In addition to collecting oral data, I acquired documents (always on request), took photographs and made diagrams of the spatial arrangement of objects. Fieldnotes were typed up each day by myself. Throughout I have used pseudonyms for place-names, institutions and people. Throughout, too, I have sought to understand the actions of staff according to my conceptual framework, and I make no claims to criticize, evaluate or to prescribe for them. Clearly it is important to allay any suspicions that one is there to inspect, to pass judgement. Nevertheless, when the findings are presented for discussion, there is the possibility that some staff may use them in an evaluatory manner, either of themselves or of others. And equally, the researchers themselves may have cause to ponder their own practice, having had the benefit of the views of the staff.

Finally, no study of only three institutions allows us to make generalizations. We need to know if, elsewhere, similar patterns exist, and if the explanations offered here are justified. As stated, the nursery schools here are Scottish. In order to refine our understanding, cross-cultural studies that hold constant the social composition of catchment areas might usefully be undertaken. Studies such as this, therefore, represent only the beginnings of the sociology of early education. The fieldwork was undertaken by myself between August 1985 and December 1986. The findings were discussed with staff in February 1988 and intermittently thereafter.

NOTES AND REFERENCES

1. Bernstein, B. 'Class and pedagogies: visible and invisible' (1975). In Bernstein, B. (ed.) *Class, Codes and Control*, Volume III. 2nd edition. London: Routledge & Kegan Paul, 1977, p 35.
2. Hartley, D. 'Some consequences of teachers' definitions of boys and girls in two infant schools'. Exeter: Unpublished PhD thesis, University of Exeter, 1977.
3. Flanders, N. A. *Analyzing Teacher Behavior*. New York: Addison-Wesley, 1970.
4. Berger, P., Berger, B. and Kellner, H. *The Homeless Mind*. Harmondsworth: Penguin, 1973.
5. Rist, R. C. 'Student social class and teacher expectations: the self-fulfilling prophecy in ghetto education'. *Harvard Educational Review*, **40**, 411–51, 1970; and Rist, R. C. *The Invisible Children: School Integration in American Society*. Cambridge, MA: Harvard University Press.
6. Kanter, R. 'The organisation child: experience management in a nursery school'. *Sociology of Education*, **45** (2), 186–212, 1972; and Lubeck, S. *Sandbox Society: Early Education in Black and White America — A Comparative Ethnography*. London: Falmer Press, 1985.
7. Hartley, op. cit. (2); King, R. 'The man in the Wendy House: researching infants' schools'. In Burgess, R. G. (ed.) *The Research Process in Educational Settings: Ten Case Studies*. Lewes: Falmer Press, 1984; and King, R. *All Things Bright and Beautiful?* London: Wiley, 1978.
8. Pollard, A. 'Coping strategies and the multiplication of social differentiation in infant classrooms'. *British Educational Research Journal*, **10** (1), 33–48, 1984.
9. Hartley, D. *Understanding the Primary School*. London: Croom Helm, 1985; and Pollard, A. *The Social World of the Primary School*. London: Holt, Rinehart & Winston, 1985.
10. Armstrong, M. *Closely Observed Children*. London: Writers' and Readers'

Press, 1980; Anyon, J. 'Social class and the hidden curriculum of work'. *Journal of Education*, **162**, 67–92, 1980; Berlak, A. and Berlak, H. *Dilemmas of Schooling: Teaching and Social Change*. London: Methuen, 1981; and Nias, J. *Primary Teachers Talking: A Study of Teaching as Work*. London: Routledge & Kegan Paul, 1989.

11. Bernstein, 1975, op. cit. (1); Hartley, D., op. cit. (2, 9); King, op. cit. (7); and King, R. 'In search of the invisible pedagogy'. *Sociology*, **13**, 445–58, 1979.

12. Schutz, A. *The Phenomenology of the Social World*. London: Heinemann, 1967.

13. King, R., op. cit. (7).

14. Berger, P. and Luckmann, T. *The Social Construction of Reality*. Harmondsworth: Penguin, 1966.

15. Glaser, B. and Strauss, A. *The Discovery of Grounded Theory*. New York: Aldine, 1967.

16. Ball, S. 'Beachside reconsidered: reflections on a methodological apprenticeship'. In Burgess, op. cit. (7).

CHAPTER 4
The Nursery Schools

An underlying theme in the research was to compare state nursery education in different socio-economic areas. Accordingly, one middle-class and two working-class nurseries were selected for study. The latter were Ramsay and Castleton Nursery Schools; the former, Fieldhouse Nursery Unit. Table 4.1 provides the details of their respective complements of staff and children.

Table 4.1 Fieldhouse, Castleton, Ramsay: staff and enrolment

	Ramsay	*Castleton*	*Fieldhouse*
FT	37	20	15
AM	44	60	25
PM	44	60	25
HT	1	1	0
NT	1	1	1
NN	6	6	3

Note: FT, full-time children; AM, morning children; PM, afternoon children; HT, headteacher; NT, nursery teacher; NN, nursery nurse. The nursery teacher is under the authority of the headteacher of the primary school. Figures for nursery nurses are full-time equivalences.

Ramsay nursery school: 'fairies not ghosties'

Ramsay's catchment area is 'multiply deprived' and had been the concern of the regional council's 'multiple deprivation working party' and its attendant working groups. About 4,000 people reside there. The list of problems besetting the area in 1986 was defined as: 'unemployment', 'low income and poor money management', 'unhappy attitudes and violence', 'tenancy problems', 'social work–welfare problems', and 'education factors'.

In a 1981 report, the working party had produced a number of statistics illustrating these problems. All but 1 per cent of the population were tenants, the vast majority tenants of the local council. Forty-one per cent of households owned dogs, many of which could be seen wandering about the open-plan estate in small packs. In 1981, 42.8 per cent of those available for work were unemployed, a figure reported as 'staggeringly high' when compared to the city's average rate. Since 1981, the situation probably worsened in the area in keeping with a deteriorating trend in the city itself. According to data published in June 1987 by the regional council's careers service, there were 534 young people registered as unemployed in the city, of whom 266 were school-leavers. There were a further 1,442 on the Youth Training Scheme (YTS), a government-funded skills training programme for 16-year-olds. The number of vacancies 'on the books' was three. 'It is fair to say', the report goes on, 'that the majority of the working population are in the unskilled manual occupational bracket.' The area of Ramsay had a less than popular reputation with local employers: only 52 out of 1,479 employed locally were from Ramsay itself. When asked why, a local employer was reported to have said that 'they smelled'. Seventy-three per cent received social security payments. Of 452 students in the city's college of education in 1981, only one resided in Ramsay; of 396 full-time students in the local technical college, not one resided in the area (of the 3,675 part-time students in the same college, only 19 were Ramsay residents). Of the pre-school age-group in the area, the percentage of under-fives attending a nursery school was only 2. Indeed 81.3 per cent of the under-fives had no pre-school education whatsoever. The national figure for Scotland, for children aged 3 to 4 in 1981, was 28.0 per cent in nursery schools, just above the regional authority's average of 24.0 per cent.[1]

Nevertheless, the working party were not of the view that a 'pathological culture of poverty' marked the area: indicators of alcoholism and violent crime were not above the city average. If inadequacies existed, they were not attributable to the individual, more to the 'national socio-economic policy' and to 'inadequate services delivery'. Extrapolations from other statistical sources are worth noting. In Scotland in 1977, the infant mortality rate per 1,000 live births in social class I was 9.2; in social class V it was 21.5. Lung cancer registration rates per 100,000 in 1972–4 were 740 in social class I, and 2,888 in social class V.[2] Only three of the households sending their children to the school had a telephone. Anecdotal evidence on the school's locale supports the statistical data. A supply teacher on her first day at Ramsay summed up her impression:

> 'When I walked up here I was really shocked. At 8.30 I virtually did not see a curtain open. There was no one working. There was no one, only dogs. I've seen houses boarded up, but not on this scale.'

The headteacher remarked that her nursery school was 'the most vandalized in the city' and had even caught fire after plastic refuse bins had been ignited. Drugs, according to the headteacher, were 'peddled openly in the area'. (It was reported to me that on one house window was a 'We Don't Sell Dope' sign.) People were also said to go from house to house buying prescribed tablets. Shoplifting 'is reckoned a career here', said the headteacher. Hearsay had it that if you gave certain people the size of your clothes, then they might be able to obtain new ones from city-centre shops at a favourable price, no questions asked.

The social composition of Ramsay Nursery School reflected that of its locale; there was little 'bussing' into the area. There were 37 full-time children, aged between 3 and 5. Of these, 18 were children of single-parent families. Fifteen of these children lived with their mothers, only two of whom were in paid employment. The other three lived with their unemployed fathers. Of the 17 full-time children from two-parent families, 65 per cent came from households where both parents were unemployed. All of these full-time children met one or more of the region's priorities for pre-school provision, such as being in single-parent families, or having particular difficulties. Of the latter, for example, four children had older siblings in special education programmes; five faced 'multiple deprivation'; three had severe speech problems; three had 'definite behaviour problems'; one had 'elected mutism'; and one 'health reasons'.

There were 44 'morning children', 14 of whom came from

Table 4.2 Ramsay (R), Fieldhouse (F) and Castleton (C): social class (%)

School	I	II	IIIN	IIIM	IV	V	UE
R	0.0	0.0	3.1	4.1	12.1	7.1	73.5
C	2.8	7.7	8.4	22.4	16.1	4.9	37.1
F	14.7	30.9	14.7	30.9	5.9	0.0	2.9

Note: Data derived from school records. Social class defined using Registrar General's Classification.

single-parent families. Thirteen of the 14 children lived with their mothers, of whom 12 were unemployed. Fifty-two per cent of the two-parent, 'morning' families had both parents who were unemployed. There were 44 'afternoon children'. Of these, 22 were children of unemployed single mothers, and one of a single mother who was in manual/unskilled work. Of the remaining 21 from two-parent families, 64 per cent had fathers who were unemployed. Table 4.2 provides comparative data on the occupational structure of the families sending children to each of the three nursery schools. Just over half of the children would start primary school the next year; the remainder would do so the following year.

Ramsay is a free-standing nursery school in an area of multiple deprivation. From the 'educational aims and curriculum' section of the school's prospectus, three broad purposes can be discerned: first, that its children should *discover and experience their environment*; second, that they should *develop cognitive and motor skills so as to make the transition to primary school*; third, that they should *acquire appropriate behaviour*. Each of these purposes is now discussed in turn, mainly from the standpoint of the headteacher, Mrs Smith, whose views were obtained during the course of informal conversation.

TO DISCOVER AND EXPERIENCE THEIR ENVIRONMENT

In this respect, the school prospectus states: 'Our aim is to give young children the opportunity to expand their experiences and lead them to discover qualities and features of their environment.'

Those who manage schools in the inner city are sometimes faced with the decision of whether or not they should have their pupils 'appreciate' the symbols of the deprivation which typifies 'their environment'. The 'environment' of Ramsay was independently defined by a local government working group:

> From the survey itself you can see the main areas that the people identified where improvements could be made to the environment. A general feeling throughout the survey seemed to be that something had to be done to control the number of dogs that wandered around the streets, the blame being put on the owners. From the total number . . . of households surveyed we found 41% owned dogs. There was also a large proportion of people who felt that trespassing was a major problem and expressed a desire for more fencing. Mention was also made of the lack of play facilities for young children, facilities for teenagers; one tenant also mentioned police apathy. A number of tenants thought that Ramsay would be improved if the Council stopped using it as a 'dumping ground'. It is also important to point out that some of the people said that they were very happy living in Ramsay and would not choose to live anywhere else.

The survey also revealed that 40 per cent of households reported dampness and 22.2 per cent problems with vandalism. Bin size and collection were regarded as unsatisfactory by about 25 per cent of those surveyed.

It was said of the Ramsay children that:

> 'Most of the children stay around the doorstep. When shoes are bought, the children don't normally go into town to the shop — the shoes are brought home.'

Ramsay was the only nursery school where 'the environment' was screened out by the use of net curtains over all of the windows. The curtains had been sent by the regional authority (though not for that reason), and new ones would shortly be requested. Nor did the children play outside on the tarmacadam play area (for reasons to be discussed in Chapter 6). There were, however, occasional trips to the countryside, and house-plants were in abundance in the school — I counted sixty-five — and 'bushes, trees and flowers' were wanted for the playground. Mrs Smith's purpose appeared to be to *protect* her children from the 'environment', rather than to help them 'discover its features and qualities'. This was revealed informally:

> *Mrs Smith*: For our children? They should be happy. Some of the [tragic] things we hear — the mind boggles. (For example, some children were under so much danger that they were not allowed access to their parents by law. While the child was in the nursery, he or she was literally under Mrs Smith's protection.)

The children were to be 'protected', 'to be given a positive attitude', to have their 'confidence built up'. For example, there were more cuddly toys at Ramsay than elsewhere, and the children came more readily to staff for a cuddle:

> *Supply teacher*: A larger percentage want to be close to you, for comfort.

Or take the case of Hallowe'en. Lest the children be upset by a surfeit of spooks, witches and 'ghosties', 'fairies' were introduced to 'balance' the 'horrors' of Hallowe'en: 'We put up a witch, but it's a happy witch!' In some nurseries, parents were asked to bring in a birthday cake for their child, but at Ramsay this could not be relied upon and the practice was not encouraged, so as to avoid disappointment for the child whose parent could not bring one. The full-time children did not have a post-lunch sleep because Mrs Smith did not like her children to wake up and 'find mummy not there'. Finally, Mrs Smith had suspended the giving of milk to the children in the wake of the Chernobyl reactor incident, though no official directive to this effect had been issued. We turn now to Mrs Smith's second formal purpose:

TO DEVELOP COGNITIVE AND MOTOR SKILLS

If Ramsay's children were seen to be in need of 'protection', so also were they to be prepared cognitively for the primary school:

> At Ramsay Nursery School we offer first-hand learning experiences by providing situations which encourage the children to pursue their natural curiosity and which help them develop language, thinking ability and physical skills. The children make contact with different adults and learn to mix with other children, thus permitting a smooth transition from home to primary school.

The preparation required was considerable: 'five out of ten children' required speech therapy. (Part of Mrs Smith's explanation of the children's poor level of oracy was her 'dummy theory': too many children spent too long sucking a dummy, thereby rendering them literally speechless.) Thus it was that, by the age of five, Mrs Smith estimated that her children were 'a year behind' their counterparts at Drummond Nursery School, which was a 'nice working class' area. Moreover, the results of the school's endeavours to provide the necessary linguistic and cognitive skills for their five-year-olds were less successful than hitherto:

Nursery teacher: It used to be that they had the basics on leaving . . . number, colour . . . but less so now.

The despondency was all the greater because the school regarded itself as materially deprived of resources, rather like its environment. For example, a number of computers had become available for nursery schools, but none had come Ramsay's way:

Nursery teacher: Why should the toffs get one [a computer]? 'It's only Ramsay' [officialdom would say] . . . We're the only school who lost insurance money on a fire.

The staff, too, were mindful of how the local primary school would see their 'graduates'. There was much talk of the 'primary one test' administered by the primary school to incoming pupils. (In Scotland, the first year of primary education is known as Primary One. A parent had been overheard saying that her child 'had passed the primary one test'.) But if the nursery school were to emphasize 'the basics' it would, said Mrs Smith, 'take the naturalness away' from the child — it would, so to say, de-child the child, as she defined it. In any event, this 'naturalness' would soon be lost when Mrs Smith's children went to the local primary school, where there was said to be 'lots of shouting' (by the teachers), where the classrooms were closed, where there were 'no decorations', and where it was both 'sombre' and 'not welcoming'.

Finally, Mrs Smith's third stated aim:

TO ACQUIRE APPROPRIATE BEHAVIOUR

Mrs Smith: Even in Ramsay we have a broad band of normality, but sometimes there's something wrong.

Just as many children were seen to be bereft of 'the basics', so too were they in need of 'the social graces', the demeanour known as 'normal'. These social graces included those of personal hygiene and safety, more of which later. They were not to be imposed, but to be taught tacitly, and always with a view to preserving the child's naturalness. In summary, Ramsay's purpose was to balance the natural innocence of the child with the purpose of inculcating the 'social graces' and providing a basis for primary school entrance. All this had to be done in a manner which protected the child from the perceived trials and tribulations of a deprived environment. Before we proceed to the other working-class nursery, Castleton, it is worth noting that, historically, the provision of nursery education in Britain has been based on a perceived need to ameliorate the adverse material conditions in deprived, urban areas. It is only relatively recently that wider access to nursery provision for all social classes has been officially endorsed. Thus we find it said, in the 1920s, 1930s and 1950s, that nursery schools should serve the poorest children. For example, in the 1920s the Nursery Schools Association (NSA) argued:

The demolition of condemned buildings is at present opening up congested areas; the inhabitants of these houses are being transferred to suburban districts; thus in two ways unique opportunities are offered for obtaining sites for Nursery Schools; it is therefore an urgent matter that Local Authorities should be induced in all their constructive plans to take account of the special needs and special claims of the pre-school child.[3]

The Hadow Report of 1933 takes a similar line:

More recently it has been recognised that other conditions — bad housing, overcrowding, etc. — often make the home an unsatisfactory environment for the young child, and that young mothers often lack the necessary knowledge how to train them.[4]

Lastly, in the egalitarian aftermath of the Second World War, similar sentiments were echoed by the Scottish Education Department:

The nursery school is of special value to children living in industrial areas, in flats and houses without gardens, in homes where the mother is delicate, where only one parent is alive, where the child is an only one, where the child is in the sole charge of elderly guardians, where the relationship between the parents is an unhappy one, where the mother is overwhelmed with domestic duties or has to go out to work.[5]

This same concern for the welfare of the child is repeated in the 1967 Plowden Report, with its call for the expansion of nursery provision in the Educational Priority Areas (EPAs). (The Scottish counterpart to Plowden, known as the 'Primary Memorandum', curiously has nothing to say about nursery education.[6]) It was in this egalitarian climate that Ramsay had been built, as had our second nursery, Castleton, to which we now turn.

Castleton nursery school: 'safe, happy, all-round development'

Ramsay and Castleton nursery schools are identical in their architecture, having been built in 1972. The catchment area of Castleton was less socially homogeneous than Ramsay's, both ethnically and in terms of social class. According to the headteacher's estimate, 30 per cent were registered as being unemployed in Castleton. When the school had been built, the levels of deprivation had been greater than of late, and one part of its catchment area, Wildwood, had had a reputation not unlike that now attracted by Ramsay. In order to illustrate the existence of poverty, the headteacher, Mrs Chalmers, recalled an occasion 'when the whole place [i.e. the school] reeked' and she had asked the parents of two of the children to wash them. The parents had reminded her of the cost of immersion heaters and she therefore had advised the use of handbasins, not baths. She remarked to her astonishment how well some children coped with deprivation, noting that some parents in Wildwood wanted 'to be normal', but lived in fear of being victimized for appearing to be so. Racism was allegedly not uncommon in the area. Six places at the school had been reserved for the Vietnamese 'boat people', but she said that they had stayed away, fearing racism, though not at the nursery school. Among her staff, the consensus was that the area was 'getting better', the evidence being that some families who had been housed in a housing 'scheme' to the south of the city were now endeavouring to move 'up', and back, to the very area where they had been housed originally. Nevertheless, the school was still subjected to acts of vandalism, and the local authority had erected a high fence around it in order to prevent this.

The social class of the children, as defined occupationally, was more varied than at Ramsay. There were 20 full-time children, three-quarters of whom were eligible for 'free meals', and only three of whose parents were employed. Just one 'full-time' family was an 'owner-occupier', and only four had a telephone. Only 11 of Castleton's 140 children came from single-parent families. When compared to Ramsay, Castleton's enrolment lies more within the skilled working class (Table 4.2). Parents were more likely to own their own homes.

Although Castleton's catchment area was more socially mixed than that of Ramsay, it was, as Table 4.2 reveals, predominantly working class. Its declared purpose was decidedly more academic:

> Our special concern is the development of speech and language, the encouragement of an appreciation of books and stories, and the development of pre-reading, pre-number and pre-writing skills. (School Prospectus)

All this was to be achieved in a 'warm, friendly, caring and stimulating atmosphere'. Perhaps an indicator of the cognitive emphasis at Castleton was the preferred use of the Keele Assessment Programme by the nursery teacher.[7] Her counterpart at Ramsay expressed doubts about Keele:

> 'I don't think I'm qualified to use Keele. You do it for the psychologist who may, or may not, retest. Some HMIs don't believe in Keele; some do. Some HMIs complained that colours, shapes and size were done, but then asked why Keele wasn't being used!'

Mrs Chalmers, who had been in post since the school opened, put stress on standard procedures:

> 'I agitate to the staff: "We must keep to our routine." '

She attracted YTS trainees who helped in the school. She insisted, however, that the trainees, when in the school, spoke 'correctly' lest their language be a bad example for the children. Lines of role and spatial demarcation were more clearly defined at Castleton, compared to Ramsay. For example, the headteacher at Ramsay usually wore an overall whereas her counterpart did not. (The local authority provided overalls only for nursery nurses.) The 'full-time' children were in a separate classroom; at Ramsay they were not. Caution and safety were major concerns of the headteacher. Castleton was the only nursery where a nursery nurse was continuously on 'bathroom duty'. Thus, when compared to Ramsay, there was less emphasis on the 'naturalness' of the children: there was more routine and ritual; more teaching and assessment; and more hierarchy and formality.

Fieldhouse nursery unit: 'an absolute guddle'

The provision of state-funded nursery education has been traditionally related to the degree of material deprivation. Ramsay and Castleton are part of that tradition. By the 1960s, however, the Plowden Report sought to extend provision in England and Wales more widely, albeit on a half-time basis.[8] In Scotland, this sentiment was echoed.[9] However, the provision of full-time nursery education was resisted, on the grounds that wherever possible the child should be with his or her mother in the early, formative years. Plowden endorsed both Piaget's influence on pedagogy and the egalitarian ideals of Margaret McMillan, whose ideals were very much compensatory and akin to Plowden's philosophy of positive discrimination.[10] The third nursery in the study, Fieldhouse, had little to compensate its children for. Fieldhouse was organizationally part of a primary school. Its nursery unit was purpose-built, set in its own large grassy and treed area known as 'the woods'. Of the three nurseries its social class composition was the highest (Table 4.2): 'There are not many artisans', as a nursery nurse put it. Attendance rates hovered about 95 per cent, these being attributed to the fact that most children arrived by car. Its locale was that of the prosperous suburb where owner-occupiers were the norm. Its setting was in a quiet cul-de-sac. Its buildings were modern and warm. No dogs roamed the streets in packs; no cars lay derelict in the road; no windows were boarded up; no pavement remained unswept; no high fence contained the nursery. Inside, no toothbrushes and face-cloths were provided for the children (as at Ramsay).

I had been forewarned of what Fieldhouse might be like. A nursery nurse at Castleton referred to the teacher-in-charge, Miss Foot, as 'very artsy-craftsy'. And so it proved. The amount of floor, window, ceiling and wall space adorned with the children's work was far greater. If some nursery teachers preferred a 'tidy appearance', Miss Foot liked 'an absolute guddle — that's what I like to see. That's how it should be'. (A 'guddle' is a mess, or muddle.) This was not to say that Miss Foot was unorganized:

> 'I like to think we're organized.'

The object of this organization was not defined in the school prospectus — Miss Foot had not written it (her predecessor had, and it had not been revised) — but, to judge from observation, Miss Foot set great store on the integration of ideas and activities, expressed as themes. While the surface symbolism of Fieldhouse might seem initially to be one of haphazard arrangement, its underlying message was one of thematic coherence. The notion of separate, discrete 'skills' to be checklisted did not figure at Fieldhouse.

The reason why the pre-school 'skills' were not stressed was because the children already had them. Most of the homes were defined as 'good' and the nursery should 'be an extension of the good home'. There were 'no problems save for a few autistic and EFL children'. Indeed, the children were 'precocious, forward, but not cheeky':

> 'We can say something quite adult to these children and they under-
> stand perfectly.'

Fieldhouse was the only nursery where tricycles and cars could be ridden *inside* the nursery; it was the only one to have pets (three goldfish and a rabbit). There was little obvious concern with reading skills:

> *Miss Foot*: We don't push them into reading — they get enough of
> that later.

But there was much concern with encouraging the children to do things for themselves, be it tidying up, taking home the pets at weekends, or 'disciplining' each other. In the words of a nursery nurse:

> 'Kids in deprived areas need more love and attention, have more physical needs — there they have a health job to do. We do an educational job.'

This neatly encapsulates the meaning behind the regional adviser's note to me after my fieldwork at Fieldhouse:

> I have made arrangements with Mrs Smith of Ramsay Nursery School for your visits. She is looking forward to welcoming you to a very different establishment from Fieldhouse.

SUMMARY

So far we have been concerned with the broad aims of each of the nurseries, relying mainly on the formal statements in the respective prospectuses and the informal comments by the head-teacher or the teacher-in-charge of the nursery unit. Although primacy has been given here to headteachers' accounts, they will later be set against those of others and against observational data. Mrs Smith at Ramsay was very aware of the need to try to balance the caring and the cognitive, the former appearing to have greater weight because the effects of the very deprived catchment area weighed heavily on her day-to-day endeavours. So it was at Castleton, the other working-class nursery school, but Mrs Chalmers, the headteacher, seemed to think that she had a better chance of setting her children on course for primary education than perhaps Mrs Smith had, possibly because the behavioural and hygiene-related basics were more in evidence at Castleton. For Mrs Chalmers, it would be a struggle, and it would require effort and enthusiasm, stimulation and routine. At Fieldhouse, the basics which Mrs Smith and Mrs Chalmers sought to build up in their children were already in place. Miss Foot at Fieldhouse could take for granted what Mrs Chalmers and Mrs Smith could not: that is, children who were well fed, articulate and had the rudiments of number, colour recognition and 'good manners'. Creativity, within the 'confines' of self-control, was sought for these children of the professional middle classes. In the garden-like setting at Fieldhouse, the metaphors of growth and nurturing — ones often applied to infant education — seemed particularly apt. Horticulture and child development were mutually reinforcing concepts.

With this background in place, we shall now try in ensuing chapters to 'filter' the procedures and practices in the three nurseries using the following frameworks. First, how is time structured? Second, what are the spatial arrangements? That is, what is the architecture and the ordering of objects? Third, how are the children's activities structured? Fourth, how is social control achieved? In considering each of these, we shall derive some indication of the degree to which they manifest bureaucracy, and how this manifestation might be related to the social class structure of the catchment area. In passing, it will become apparent that there are sometimes differences of opinion among nursery staff as to what shall count as childhood and nursery education. Evidence for these 'rifts' will be adduced, and the micro-politics of how they are contested will be discussed, mainly in Chapter 9.

NOTES AND REFERENCES

1. Scottish Education Department. 'Provision for pre-school children'. *Statistical Bulletin* **6/A2/1984**, 1984.

2. Brown, G. and Cook, R. *Scotland: The Real Divide*. Edinburgh: Mainstream Publishing, 1983, p. 209.

3. Nursery Schools Association. *Fourth Annual Report*. London: Nursery Schools Association, 1927, p. 11.

4. Hadow Report. *Report of the Consultative Committee on Infant and Nursery Schools*. London: HMSO, 1933, p. 116.

5. Scottish Education Department. *The Primary School in Scotland*. Edinburgh: HMSO, 1950, p. 127.

6. Scottish Education Department. *Primary Education in Scotland*. Edinburgh: HMSO, 1965.

7. Tyler, S. *Keele Pre-School Assessment Guide* (experimental edition). Slough: NFER, 1980.

8. Plowden Report. *Children and their Primary Schools*. London: HMSO, 1967, p. 128.

9. Scottish Education Department. *Before Five*. Edinburgh: HMSO, 1971, p. 48.

10. Lowndes, G. A. N. *Margaret McMillan: The Children's Champion*. London: Museum Press, 1960.

CHAPTER 5

The Time of their Lives

Daughter: When's my TV programme on, daddy?
Father: In five minutes.
Daughter: Is that a long time, daddy?

Rousseau encouraged educators not to set temporal limits on the activities of children. Time was theirs, not ours. It was not for us to make on their behalf. They should set the pace, not us.[1] Over the past hundred years, however, our infants have been taught that measured, clock-time is real time. The natural time of night and day, of the seasons, has gradually been replaced by finely divided units of time. Children come to realize that clock-time is natural. They develop concepts of punctuality and tardiness, of being on time. In short, children acquire a routine which can be coordinated, to the minute, to clock-time. Consider this account of the Rachel McMillan Nursery School in Deptford:

> The nursery school opens at 7.30 a.m. to admit special cases and most of the children arrive between 8 a.m. and 9 a.m. They make their way to their own shelters with a mother or an elder sister who has brought them, and after greeting their teacher go straight to the bathroom for their morning toilet. Breakfast is served at 9 o'clock. The morning is spent in handiwork occupations or in play either in the garden or in the shelter if weather is inclement. Between 11.30 a.m. and 12 noon the children sit down to a two-course dinner, after which they are ready for their midday sleep. The afternoon's activities consist of freeplay, music and games. Tea is served at 4 o'clock and between 5 and 5.20 p.m. the parents arrive to take their children home.[2]

A recent report on pre-five education in the Glasgow region noted that:

> [In nurseries] Most of the inter-action with children was undertaken by assistant teachers and nursery nurses. It was *noticeable how the use*

> *of children's time and activities in nursery schools and classes were highly
> organised and structured, which contrasted with play groups or day nurseries*
> [emphasis added].[3]

Time, therefore, is constructed for the children, not by the children. This arrangement of time becomes, for the child, a basic. As the 1933 Hadow Report puts it: 'He will soon subscribe to the daily routine as a matter of course, and will tend to do what everyone else is doing'.[4] But the concept of time, like that of childhood, is a social construction which varies across cultures and in their histories. What we come to regard as the whole child, or the nature of the child, is not a universal absolute, and may be explained sociohistorically. In Chapter 2, the theoretical insights provided by Elias were considered. The nub of his theory was that social functions have, under the pressure of competition, become ever more differentiated. The individual must increasingly attune his or her behaviour to that of others. There is a web of interconnectedness:

> The individual is compelled to regulate his conduct in an increasingly
> differentiated, more even and more stable manner.[5]

'Civilization' requires *constant* self-control. This self-repression of affects and drives requires a prolonged 'civilizing process'. The nursery school is, apart from the maternity hospital, the first social and public institution wherein the standardization of childhood begins, although, as Elias notes, 'the pattern of self-constraints, the template by which drives are moulded, certainly varies widely according to the function and position of the individual within this network'. In order to participate in this chain of interconnected social functions, great precision is required of the individual: accurate timing is crucial. To quote Elias:

> It makes people accustomed to subordinating momentary inclinations to the overriding necessities of interdependence, it trains them to eliminate all irregularities from behaviour and to achieve permanent self-control.[6]

Once an accurate instrument of time-measurement had become widely available, the possibility of keeping time and being punctual was realized. It is not, therefore, the clock itself which oppresses us, but 'the growing complexity of human interactions which is regulated by the exact measurement of time' (report of unpublished conference speech by Elias given in Buck-Morss).[7]

This raises the question of why the regulation of time at the point of industrial production should be so precise. The adage 'time is money' (or profit) is neatly encapsulated in F. W. Taylor's scientific management practice of 'time and motion' studies on the assembly line during the first two decades of this century. Earlier, in the mid-nineteenth century, entrepreneurial capitalists had lamented the dilatory and unpunctual behaviour of their employees.

'I found the utmost distaste', one hosier reported, 'on the part of the men, to any regular hours or regular habits . . . . The men themselves were considerably dissatisfied, because they could not go in and out as they pleased, and have what holidays they pleased, and go on just as they had been used to'.[8]

Hitherto, the labours of the peasantry had been in the field, not the factory. Their sense of time was seasonal and cyclical, not linear. Similarly, the labours of fishermen were limited by the ebb and flow of the tides. In entrepreneurial capitalism, time was not to be 'wasted': it was to be 'spent' productively, on the industrialist's behalf. The bureaucratic management of time, facilitated by the clock, had become essential to maximizing the time which could be allocated for manufacturing purposes. Clock time was precise (in terms of seconds, minutes and hours), accurate (by virtue of its fine mechanical specifications) and seemingly objective. Nevertheless, even the clock could be 'turned' to the industrialist's advantage:

The clocks at the factories were often put forward in the morning and back at night, and instead of being instruments for the measurement of time, they were used as cloaks for cheatery and oppression.[9]

Bureaucratic 'clock time' had to be imposed on the pre-industrial sense of time held by former peasants or cottage workers. This marks the beginning of a 'bureaucratic cognitive style', a style which included a bureaucratized sense of space, time and disposition.[10] The harsh management techniques used by 'overseers' in early factory production attest to the pervasiveness of agrarian, pre-industrial, pre-bureaucratic notions of time, space and demeanour among workers.[11] Since the 1930s, however, these rigid bureaucratic notions have been 'loosened'.[12] Consider this extract from the 1983 *Harvard Business Review*:

> For 150 years US employers and employees have taken for granted that subjection to the time clock is the price of efficiency. Now however, with more than one-fifth of the labour force functioning under flexible, compressed, or voluntarily reduced work schedules, some employers have gone so far as to toss out time clocks, shred time cards, and take a new look at the nine-to-five day and the five-day week.[13]

This structural 'looseness' derives mainly from the industrial psychology movement emanating from the Hawthorne Studies in the USA during the late 1920s. The beginnings of this movement arose out of the worker's reaction against the authoritarian strictures of Taylorism, and capitalism's concern to avert worker unrest. There was a need to produce an accord between the interests of both worker and employer:

> The peril of a situation in which falling wages and unemployment on an unprecedented scale are leading features which drive the more active-minded employers to make considerable concessions from the old capitalist autocracy. . . . From the employer's standpoint the problem is one of devising adequate and reliable stimuli to draw from the workers a longer and more regular output of productive energy, a greater willingness to adopt and apply new mechanical and business methods, and, in general, to co-operate more effectively with the other factors of production.[14]

The ensuing human relations managerial approach paid some heed to the imputed social and psychological needs of workers, but only to the extent that these worker needs did not conflict with, or replace, the central need of management, namely to maximize profit.

An example of this structural looseness is the spatial arrangement known as open-plan; another, relevant here, is the temporal arrangement known as 'flexi-time'. These spatial and temporal weakenings of the work-setting appear, superficially, to offer important concessions to the worker. But it can be argued that they allow management to 'exert' more effective control. That is, in respect of 'open-plan' arrangements, the workers are now more visible, both to each other and to management. They may be more likely to control themselves — to *take responsibility for* their own action, to supervise themselves. This accords with Elias's notion of increasing *self*-control in highly differentiated social structures. Likewise, flexi-time may *appear* democratic:

> The changes in work scheduling have substantially increased employees' choices over their personal and professional lives and *have demonstrated the responsiveness of the workplace to the open, democratic society in which it functions* [emphasis added].[15]

In open-plan settings, workers can supervise each other. Under flexi-time regimes, self-monitoring, aided by programmable digital watches, is technologically facilitated, thereby allowing the worker some opportunity to reschedule official time. Similarly, at home, he can reschedule the packaged television programme slots by continually changing channels, or by video-taping portions of them.

Theories of management must incorporate two competing ideals: that of profitability; and that of the democratic notion of individual choice. The human relations managerial approach generated terms riddled with the latter: 'worker participation' and 'individual needs', to state two. But, at root, the industrial psychology movement of the 1920s was a managerial response to rigid bureaucratic work structures which were becoming increasingly disliked by workers. Since that time, capitalism has had to balance its primary goal of profit against increasingly self-centred attitudes on the part of workers. Such self-centredness is part of the 'me-too', consumerist ethic which capitalism requires of the individual-as-*consumer*. However, this same self-centredness may be *contrary* to capitalism's expectations of the individual-as-*producer*. The trade-off is that the individual-as-producer will be given space or time at work for his or her 'me-too', self-centred needs to be met, but only in so far as these needs do not undermine profit levels. Thus the employee's *choices* at work (as long as they further productivity) can be defined as meeting *democratic* criteria, at the same time as meeting the needs of business.

The trend towards flexi-time is increasing. According to the US Bureau of Labor Statistics, 11.9 per cent of full-time, non-farm wage salary workers were on flexi-time, and it is estimated that 15 to 20 per cent of US employers offer flexi-time, mainly in white-collar work settings.[16] The managerial efficiency of flexi-time is not yet clearly established: employee attitudes and behaviour have improved but flexi-time's effects on levels of productivity have shown no clear trends. What is interesting for the purpose of this study is that we may be witnessing a convergence of 'nursery time' and 'work-time' (especially in the white-collar, service sector). Both weaken the bureaucratic concept of fixed times for activities, but they do so for different reasons. That is to say, the notion of nursery school time for children derives mainly from those continental European philosophers of education such as Rousseau who advocated 'freedom' and choice for the individual as part of a liberal, romantic view of the child. On the other hand, the new work-based flexi-time has been introduced to render employment palatable to employees who may increasingly be seeking more self-fulfilment and personal dignity at work.

Flexi-time is part of a wider consideration of change and permanence in society. Stonier argues that the 'future', itself a concept associated with modernity, will be marked by increasing rates of change.[17] Life will be less predictable; a new sense of uncertainty will prevail, perhaps exemplified by the uncertainty of paid employment. We may need to be able to switch more readily from a sense of 'work-time' to 'free-time'. Whatever sense of time is required in an interconnected, complex society, young children will have to learn it, and to regard it as natural. In the nursery school there are usually no bells. The clocks are for the teachers, not the children. Nevertheless, the child's sense of time is tacitly structured: the child begins to acquire a sense of *sequence* of events, and these may be referred to as 'times', such as 'music time' or 'going-home-time'. How is time classified and arranged in the nursery school? Whose definition of time prevails: the teacher's or the child's? How much temporal freedom is allowed the child in the face of society's bureaucratic cognitive style? These questions are now considered.

In some manuals on pre-school practice, the notion of bureau-cratized 'routine' time is taken for granted. (In passing, it is noteworthy that all three nurseries here actually categorized their children on the basis of time: that is, morning children, afternoon children, full-time children.) Take, for example, the manual *Young Children in Action: A Manual for Pre-school Education*. The reader is told:

> Children need to be aware of the daily routine and know the names of its parts so that they don't go through the day wondering what's going to happen next or worrying that they won't get a chance to go outside and play on the swings.[18]

These 'parts' should preserve the same sequence each day. The 'elements' of a daily routine are defined as: planning time, work time, clean-up time, recall, snack and small-group time, outside time, circle time.[19] Moreover, the bureaucratic notion of moni-toring is stressed:

> Some teaching teams find it helpful to jot down observations during work time so they'll be able to remember everything as they *plan* and *evaluate*.
> Some teaching teams put large *file* cards and a pencil in an area . . . other teams use *clip boards* and paper, while still others carry small file cards about in their pockets. [emphasis added][20]

There is, therefore, in this brief extract the unexamined assump-tion that the child's sense of time should be structured into these 'parts', or 'elements of a routine'. Activities, or 'times', should be routine, predictable and orderly. They should be monitored, observed, recorded and evaluated. These procedures are justified lest the children 'lose' themselves:

> Between certain segments of the daily routine there are transitions a teaching team needs to think about and plan for. As children move from one activity to the next, *they can easily lose control of themselves if they don't know what to expect and what's expected of them*. [emphasis added][21]

These prescriptions for nursery schools derive from the American High/Scope curriculum, which is being introduced into some

English nursery schools.[22] The impression to be gained is one of a production process (the child proceeding through the 'times' and 'activities') which is continuously being monitored for quality control. It is very reminiscent of Taylorist time-and-motion analyses. (It is appropriate to note here that High/Scope and Head Start compensatory programmes are provided mainly for the working-class child. Lubeck provides a vivid analysis of how the regime in such a programme compared with that in a nursery setting for the children of professional parents.[23])

Let us return to the nursery schools at issue here. Consider, by way of introduction, the following extracts of children's thoughts on time:

> *Girl*: Now I am making a birthday cake [out of green playdough]
> *Nursery nurse*: Who's it for?
> *Girl*: You.
> *Nursery nurse*: Are you going to put candles on it?
> *Girl*: One.
> *Nursery nurse*: I think I'm a little older than one!

In this exchange, the child is expected to change from a make-believe reality (making a 'birthday cake' out of playdough) to a real, temporal reality (knowing that the nursery nurse is X years old and that this should be represented numerically by X candles on the 'cake'). Some children had a greater knowledge of time than adults:

> *Jane*: My mum said it's Sunday.
> *Alice*: It's not.
> *Jane*: And it isn't is it? She's always wrong!

For all pre-school children, their sense of time is rendered linear, sequential and regular. Events are defined as 'times' and are attached to particular 'activities', often in particular 'areas'. Children whose sense of time lacks this structure are said to be 'lost'. At Castleton I was shown the instructions for staff on the theme of 'Our Nursery School'. It said:

Discuss the nursery school day:
Arrival — free play — juice-time — outdoor play — 'band' — music
time — story-time — A.M. home-time — lunch
Discuss time in the nursery school in general terms rather than specific time:
Morning — late morning — afternoon — midday — midmorning —
sequence of events.

This degree of written formalization of times was not evident
elsewhere. What was common was the children's awareness of
'tidy-up time' about 9.45 each morning, prior to 'snack-time'. It
was as if a message to this effect had been subconsciously trans-
mitted around the three nursery schools. The children could not
'tell the time' on the clock, but they knew that 'snack-time' was
imminent, or at least next in the sequence of events. They could,
for example, learn to recognize the clues of an impending time
change: the rearrangement of furniture and partitions which
preceded juice-time.

The ways in which the children structured their 'times' turned
on how their teachers and nursery nurses arranged them. These
'times' varied little across the three nurseries, as Appendix II
reveals. Each 'time' had its own sequence of events. It varied
within and between schools, but not by much. To illustrate this,
take 'snack' or 'juice' time. Here was a 'time' which occurred at
the same hour each day in each school, but which was interpreted
differently. We begin with Ramsay.

Ramsay: 'snack-time'

The 'yellow group' sits behind the piano with Mrs Fletcher. All
are seated on the floor, in an arc. A nursery nurse brings out
the jug of juice. The partitions on the open-plan area remain open.
(Each colour group had the same coloured beakers, face-cloths,
toothbrushes and table napkins. I did not see toothbrushes and
face-cloths in the other nursery schools, and this may reflect
Ramsay's greater 'hygiene' role.)

Mrs Fletcher: Did your mummy give you ten bob? (She brings
out a money box with cardboard coins in it.) Show me your ten

bob. (A child had mistakenly referred to a fifty-pence piece as 'ten bob'.)

Fiona: I spent it!

Mrs Fletcher: You're still not sitting . . . sitting means putting your bottom on the carpet . . . You're *still* not sitting (a little boy was kneeling in the cramped space).

Mrs Fletcher moves around the group on her knees, dispensing an unpeeled segment of orange to each child. As they eat this, she pours out a diluted orange drink into blue beakers. Two children break ranks from the arc.

Mrs Fletcher: Where are you going? Sit back. (Each child says 'thank you' on being served.)

Mrs Fletcher: Right, now *I* can sit down.

The children chatter away as they have their juice. When they have finished they return their beaker to Mrs Fletcher, who stacks it.

Again at Ramsay, consider Miss Fauld's 'snack-time'. She had trained under an apparently very formal headteacher. This headteacher had allegedly:

locked the doors and no one was allowed in after hours. When she came out of the office everyone went rigid with fear.

So, Miss Faulds had been exposed professionally both to the relatively more easy-going Mrs Smith and to a very formal mentor. Her conduct at 'snack-time' suggests the influence of both, as the following reveals.

The previous day the children had been taken out into the countryside. The 'nature table' was scattered with nests, rocks, twigs, a mouse's skull and a live ladybird, all of which had been collected. As aids to viewing them, some magnifying glasses were made available. Immediately before snack-time some of the children had been examining the collection.

Miss Faulds: It's tidy-up time. You can come back after your juice.

Sit down in your corner. Right then everyone — sorry and all that!
(She sits them down in a circle beside the nature table and counts
the children.) One blue one missing . . . Jane.

Miss Faulds: Who's sitting nice and quietly?

She looks at Hamish:

Miss Faulds: Who's had their hair cut?!! I saw your brother yesterday
and he said you'd had it cut!

A little girl, Linda, serves the children a cream-filled biscuit.
On reaching one child, Alan, she turns disdainfully to Miss
Faulds:

Linda: Alan stinks!

Miss Faulds: Don't tell him he stinks!

Miss Faulds returns to the kitchen to refill the juice jug, leaving
the children to their snack. On her return the children are com-
mended for their behaviour during her absence:

Miss Faulds: That was very good. Quiet talking's O.K. — it's when
you start shouting . . . Right. On your bottoms. Dean, you've finished
your biscuit. Come and get your juice.

The children come out, one by one, for juice.

Miss Faulds: You're not supposed to take it [the biscuit] apart. Eat
it up! We'll wait till everyone's finished and then we'll have a
colour. Put your cups on the floor in front of you if you think you're
finished. All people wearing red bring your cups up . . .

At this point, some children turn to the nature table behind them,
but they are reminded that it is still 'juice-time'.

Miss Faulds: All those wearing blue bring their cups up. . . . Right, let
me hear you sing. I don't want silly singing . . . 'In a cottage in a wood,
a little girl by the window stood . . .'

During the singing, she moves Hamish away from the nature table. He is reluctant. Spontaneously, Miss Faulds integrates 'juice-time' and another activity:

'I know a song about a ladybird' (like the one on the nature table).

She teaches them the song, picks up the ladybird, sings to them about it, and they come up to her and look at it on her hand. What began, therefore, as a tightly controlled 'juice-time' was loosened by the teacher's response to the children's interest in their nature table.

Finally at Ramsay, I observed Mrs Smith at 'juice-time'. The children sit on the floor in the 'music room', a closed room. Lindsay hands out the snack:

Mrs Smith: Say thank-you to Lindsay for handing out the biscuits.

Mrs Smith pours out the juice, but is interrupted by a boy who comes across and gives her his half-eaten biscuit:

Mrs Smith: Didn't you like it? . . . you come and get your juice. (To all.) If you've finished your biscuits, come and get your juice off the table . . . I've got trainers on. (In fact, they were blue, red and white leather shoes.) What colour are they? . . . blue . . . and red stripes as well.

I'll put out the tray there [on the floor]. If you're finished, put your mug on the tray. If you want more, I'll come round in a minute (with more juice).

Would you like to sing for us? (No response.) Craig's going to sing us a song (but he forgets it). Do you know a nursery rhyme then? . . . Humpty Dumpty! . . . Shall we help him? (They all recite 'Humpty Dumpty'.)

After this, boys and girls alternate to come and stand beside Mrs Smith to sing or to narrate a story. As they did so, they received a cuddle.

What was interesting about Mrs Smith's 'juice-time', apart from the fact that she actually conducted one — her counterpart at Castleton did not do this — was its lack of formality (no tellings off, but cuddles for the children) compared to the school regimes of Miss Faulds and Mrs Fletcher. This very variation of what counted as 'juice-time' at Ramsay is indicative of the flexible approach of Mrs Smith, an approach reputedly very much at odds with that of her predecessor. It was an approach, too, which differed from the practice at Castleton, whose architecture was identical to Ramsay's, and whose catchment area was also working class, though less deprived.

Castleton: 'juice-time'

Juice-time (not snack-time) at Castleton constituted the turning point of the morning. Before, it had been badge-time, choosing-time and tidy-up time; after came toilet-time, play-time (while the staff had their break) and play-time outside (weather permitting) or music, all followed by getting-ready-for-home time, which included story-time, the children's giving up their badges, putting on their coats and collecting their paintings, etc.

'Juice-time' at Castleton was more formal than at Ramsay. First, the partitions were drawn across the open areas, for privacy. (The open 'areas' at Castleton were distinguished from the closed 'full-time room'; at Ramsay, the open 'areas' were distinguished from the closed 'music room'.) Here the staff were mindful of Mrs Chalmers' 'routine'. Part of her policy, not followed at Ramsay, was to keep the 'full-time children' in a separate room, at that time with Mrs Turner and Miss Bond. (Mrs Turner would have been very much at one with Mrs Smith's 'protection' philosophy at Ramsay because they both dealt with the most disadvantaged children by showing them affection.) The full-time children brought their own juice to the nursery. If they forgot, they had water, which was said to be much better for them anyway. Whereas their counterparts in the areas could consume a whole beaker or carton of juice, the full-time children had to make do with half in the morning and the other half in the afternoon.

Mrs Turner: It's nearly juice-time. . . . Who left the jigsaw unfinished. Hazel? You must finish it . . . .If you're in difficulty, ask. (Mrs Turner helps her to finish it.)

Mrs Turner's colleague, Miss Bond, is cutting up an apple at her table.

Mrs Turner: Five minutes to juice-time. Wash your hands, Alex. We'll have to get tidied up now.

Meanwhile, Miss Bond puts her arm round Colin and helps him 'halve the apple'. At 9.50, the 'full-time' children sit at two tables, with a nursery nurse at each, and receive their juice and apple segment. They discuss the weather, the day of the week, and 'news'. After 'juice' comes 'toilet-time' in the continuously monitored bathrooms.

In the 'areas', 'juice-time' with Miss Yates was more structured. The children were divided on the basis of sex, one sitting on chairs, the other on mats, the arrangement alternating each day.

Miss Yates: Get your hands washed and go to your corners please. Boys on chairs, girls on mats (arranged in a semi-circle). Linda, there's an extra chair because you've been so good. (Michelle, however, was not happy with just a mat.) Michelle won't enjoy her juice today . . . she'll have to stand.

The children were called to order, being asked to sit, cross-legged, with hands on knees. Meanwhile, James counts the children for juice: 'thirteen, good'. 'Will all the boys stand up?' (to be counted). 'Will all the girls stand up?' (to be counted). 'Will you tell me how many girls we have?' Miss Yates's more 'educational' and formal 'juice-time' is in contrast with the friendlier informality afforded the (mainly deprived) 'full-time' children. The sex differentiation and oblique social control evident in Miss Yates's 'group' was missing in the 'full-time room'.

Juice-time could be regarded in a number of ways: as a calming-down period after choosing-time; as an opportunity for a little formal instruction about time and weather ('Friday's the last day of your week.' 'This is September and it's autumn when the leaves start to turn brown.'); as an informal register-taking; as a time to tidy the nursery; and as an opportunity for the staff to retreat to the private space of the staffroom. Juice-time never varied, and the pre-juice-time routine of tidying up gave the children forewarning of it. A sense of urgency was given to the children:

'Go and tidy up our corner, Hazel. It's juice-time. Hurry up!'

There was never any question of *not* having a fixed time for juice or a snack in any of the nurseries. It was seen as an integrating ritual.

Fieldhouse: snack-time

Earlier, in respect of snack-time at Ramsay, I have noted that Miss Faulds had spontaneously integrated snack-time with the objects on the nature table. At Ramsay and Castleton, this integration of other activities with snack-time or juice-time was rare. At Fieldhouse it was not: that is, although snack-time was timetabled as a discrete activity, *substantively* it was always linked thematically to 'non-snack' activities. The extract below illustrates the point.

At Fieldhouse, pre-snack 'tidy-time' was at 9.55 a.m. This meant that the children swept up, mopped the floors and put away everything that had been on the tables and floor. They then assembled in the two large areas. In both areas the tables (two of them) were brought together, the children sat down, and one of them would be assigned to walk round the tables counting the number of children. Sometimes they would all count together:

Nursery nurse: Let's count together . . . how many on that table? Eight. On this one, six, but here comes Alice, so there's seven!

A 'bus-cake' was brought in as part of the current 'transport' theme. The children and nursery nurses proceeded to analyse the shape of the buses. They then reviewed the recipe they had followed in making it.

Nursery nurse: Now, someone who's very strong . . . (The children raise their hands. Jim hands out the cake and slice of apple.)

I think we'll have our snack, and then we'll have news time. If you cough, blow or sneeze, use a hanky if you please!!

The people on this table are nearly finished. . . . I'm looking for someone to wash up . . . Peter . . . who's sitting nicely. Peter, choose someone to dry, and don't leave bubbles in the bottom of the cup. (The children then move to the story mat to sing a song 'about a bus', thereby integrating it with the transport theme.)

While snack-time at Fieldhouse temporally divided the morning, it did not divide the morning's activities. Discussion was not usually only about the day of the week, or the seasons. The children were assumed to know these:

(While sitting having their snack, a child noticed the absence of one of the group, reporting it to Miss Foot):
Miss Foot: Maybe tomorrow he'll be back.
Child: He'll not be back tomorrow.
Miss Foot: Why not?
Child: It's Saturday!

What also distinguished Fieldhouse was the expectation that the children themselves tidy up, dispense the snack (milk, fruit, cheese rather than biscuits), and wash up afterwards. They needed very little reminding of the procedures. On one occasion in my early visits, I noted: 'They all sit down automatically, ready (for snack)'. They were more likely to control themselves than be directed by staff. Snack-time enabled the children to show their civilized behaviour, as Elias would have termed it. They were not seen as 'babies', in need of a cuddle, as in the full-time room at Castleton, or at Ramsay. Indeed, mothers and others who 'babied them' were regarded as a little different:

'The mothers sometimes baby them, but then you see them [the children] in the street and realize how tiny they are'.

These children were seen as, and expected to be, grown up. Snack-time provided a setting for them to display this behaviour, formally, to the staff and to each other.

SUMMARY

The notion of being lost has a spatial connotation. But if someone is 'all over the place', or 'lost', when at work, it normally does not refer to his geographical meanderings. It implies an absence of clear direction, of ineffective time-management. The shift towards flexi-time in the workplace requires a precise, *inner* sense of time, one which replaces the reminders provided hitherto by horns, hooters and bells. The former develops an *individual* management of time; the latter organizes large groups in time, and on time. To facilitate the development of our inner sense of time, we can program our wrist-watches and telephones to emit a sound at a given time. We can attend the ever-burgeoning series of time-management courses. And we can buy our very own computerized, *personal* organizer. Increasingly we must monitor and manage *ourselves*. All this is part and parcel of Elias's discussion of self-control and regulation. It will be recalled that Elias argued that self-regulation will tend to occur last among the poorest, oppressed groups. In the nurseries in the study here, only Castleton approximated the more traditionally bureaucratic management of time. Even so, although there was a similarity of times across the nurseries, these times did not contain the same activities, even though they may have been labelled the same, such as snack-time. In all of the nurseries, times and sequences were fixed, not flexible. (In using the term 'bureaucratic', I am doing so to describe a style of organizing. No value judgement is being imputed.) Little discretion was afforded the child about *when* he or she could, say, take a snack, or come in, or go out. Time was for the staff, not the child, to 'make'. Despite the references to freedom, play and choosing, the nursery school sets these notions within carefully defined time allocations. There is routine, and its elements rarely change, either in order or in duration. Slowly but surely, the children cease to get temporally 'lost': they tacitly acquire our sense of 'clock time'. Spontaneity begins to ebb away from their 'nature'.

NOTES AND REFERENCES

1. Rousseau, J.-J. *Emile*, translated by B. Foxley, London: Dent, 1911, p. 57.
2. Hadow Report. *Report of the Consultative Committee on Infant and Nursery Schools*. London: HMSO, 1933, p. 255.
3. Strathclyde Regional Council. *Under Fives*. Glasgow: Strathclyde Regional Council, 1985.
4. Hadow Report, op cit. (2), p. 120.

5. Elias, N. *The Civilizing Process.* Volume 2, *State Formation and Civilization*, translated by E. Jeffcott. Oxford: Basil Blackwell, 1982, p. 232. (Originally published in 1939.)

6. Ibid., p. 248.

7. Buck-Morss, S. Review of Elias's *The Civilizing Process*, Volume 1 (Oxford: Basil Blackwell, 1978; originally published in 1939), *Telos*, **37**, 181–98, 1978.

8. Pollard, S. 'Factory discipline in the industrial revolution'. *Economic History Review*, **16**, 254–71, 1963, p. 255.

9. Anonymous, 1887, quoted in Thompson, E.P. 'Time, work-discipline and industrial capitalism'. *Past and Present*, **38**, 56–97, 1967, p. 86.

10. Berger, P., Berger, B. and Kellner, H. *The Homeless Mind.* Harmondsworth: Penguin, 1973.

11. Pollard, S. *The Genesis of Modern Management.* London: Arnold, 1965.

12. Bidwell, C.E. 'The school as a formal organization'. In March, J.G. (ed.) *A Handbook of Organizations.* New York: Rand McNally, 1965.

13. Rosow, J.M. and Zager, R. 'Punch out the time clocks'. *Harvard Business Review*, **61**, 12–30, 1983.

14. Hobson, J.A. *The Evolution of Modern Capitalism.* London: George Allen & Unwin, 1949 (originally published 1894).

15. Rosow and Zager, op. cit. (13), p. 4.

16. Ibid., p. 13.

17. Stonier, T. 'Changes in Western society: educational implications'. In Schuller, T. and Megarry, J. (eds) *The World Yearbook of Education: Recurrent Education and Lifelong Learning.* London: Kogan Page, 1979.

18. Hohmann, M., Banet, B. and Weikart, D.P. *Young Children in Action.* Ypsilanti, MI: The High Scope Press, 1979, p. 57.

19. Ibid., pp. 59–60.

20. Ibid., p. 85.

21. Ibid., p. 98.

22. Makins, V. 'Curriculum cure-all?' *Times Educational Supplement Scotland*, **1091**, 25, 1987.

23. Lubeck, S. *Sandbox Society: Early Education in Black and White America: A Comparative Ethnography.* London: Falmer Press, 1985.

CHAPTER 6

No Templates Please

Buildings are symbols of culture. The more we experience them the less we are aware that they are affecting us. Sommer puts it well: 'Our habits impel our habitations, and our habitations impel our lives.'[1] The institutional arrangements of space constitute the 'hidden dimension'.[2] Some time–space configurations are what Hall calls 'monochronic'; others are 'polychronic'.[3] The former accord with bureaucracy; the latter with more 'open' organizational forms. For example, in respect of the former, the modern high-rise office block is a physical manifestation of the social relations of a bureaucracy. Its form allows for the accommodation of a hierarchically arranged complexity of roles, each of which will have its demarcated space. The height, area and privacy of this space will correlate with the status of its occupant. This association between altitude and authority harks back to a time when surveillance by 'superiors' over 'lower participants' had to be undertaken with the naked eye. This naked-eye surveillance can now be replaced by electronic surveillance. Indeed, it is now technologically possible to replace the physical, concrete bureaucracy by information technology. But although the technology is available, the prevailing culture may not allow for it. That is, we are still pre-disposed to the physical and spatial representations of organizational forms such as bureaucracy. We are used to spaces which are rigidly defined in form and function, both at home and at work.

In the previous chapter, it was argued that the bureaucratic concept of time in the workplace is being rendered more flexible, not only because some employers regard it as being more efficient to do so, but also because it seems to meet the worker's demands for a greater say in his or her working conditions. Moreover, technologies and theories of management tend to have consequences for the ways in which individuals are arranged socially and spatially. Mass production technologies gave rise to factories and 'industrial areas'. A distinction was drawn between working and living. The rise of human relations management theory in the 1930s was intended to cater to the social and psychological needs of workers, but always with a view to greater productivity. Notions such as flexi-time, participatory decision-making, quality circles and corporate fitness programmes were all examples of this managerial startegy. So, too, was the open-plan office.

The term 'open' has a democratic ring to it. The 'open education' movement (known also as 'progressive' and 'child-centred' education) enjoyed a brief period of official support during the late 1960s, especially in primary education. Similarly, 'open-plan offices' were constructed during the same period, as were open-plan schools. The former were said to facilitate a more collaborative managerial style which drew upon the tenets of human relations management theory; the latter were said to facilitate the implementation of child-centred pedagogy. Both were cheaper to build and maintain than their cellular predecessors. Both provided a softer décor, with carpets and curtains. Both fostered notions of 'team-work' or 'team-teaching'. Both allowed for the flexible use of screens and furniture to create new spatial arrangements. Both permitted inter-personal surveillance. Both bring to mind Bentham's Panopticon, or Inspection-House, a structure (be it poor-house, prison, 'madhouse', factory or school) where any inmate could be observed without knowing it. Even if the inmate was not being observed constantly, he should, as Bentham put it, 'conceive himself to be so'.[4]

Neither the open-plan school nor its office counterpart were popular. When office workers moved to open-plan settings their satisfaction and motivation declined, with no evidence of improved productivity. The loss of privacy and the difficulty of exchanging confidences were cited as important sources of dissatisfaction.[5] And so it was in schools. There was little acceptance by teachers of open architecture.[6] It would be facile to attribute this to the 'territorial imperative'. That is, it cannot be attributable to a purely genetic propensity for the acquisition of territory, as sociobiological theory argues. This would merely pose a genetic reductionism in favour of architectural determinism. Another consideration may be offered. Teachers, particularly at secondary level, would have been professionally socialized into a bureaucratic cognitive style (for primary school teachers, this may have been less so). Further, the discipline of educational administration itself has been infused with neo-Taylorism, or scientific management theory, and this too serves to sustain the bureaucratic cognitive style in education. The architecture in which this professional socialization occurs is one of highly demarcated social spaces, rigid and permanent. The open-plan environment 'housed' this bureaucratic cognitive style. That is, teachers continued to act *as if* they were still in closed-classroom schools.[7] But this may not always occur: that is, child-centred education and open architecture *may* coincide. Neill, however, found that in the Scottish nursery schools which he studied, more openness was associated with more time spent on 'moving around, doing nothing, and in aggression and active play', all arguably child-centred activities, but not necessarily academic ones.[8] That said, consideration is now given to the relationship among architecture, organization and pedagogy in each of the three nurseries here. The approach will be as follows: first, the floor-plan of the nurseries is provided; second, the structuring of internal space is analysed; third, the overlap between 'classroom' and 'playground' spaces is discussed; fourth, the boundary relationship between nursery and home is considered.

Inside nursery spaces

We shall examine first the ways in which space was structured *inside* each nursery, beginning with the arrangements in the two working-class nurseries. The architecture of Ramsay and Castleton was identical (Figures 6.1 and 6.2). Their respective catchment areas were working class, with Ramsay's the more so. In both there was a headteacher, a nursery teacher and a group of nursery nurses. Despite this commonality of structure, environment and staffing, the perceptions of the architecture varied. Castleton's use of the open space was more bureaucratized than Ramsay's. The difference was mainly due to the more formal role structure at Castleton, which, in turn, required an associated differentiation of spaces.

77

PLAYGROUND
VERANDAH

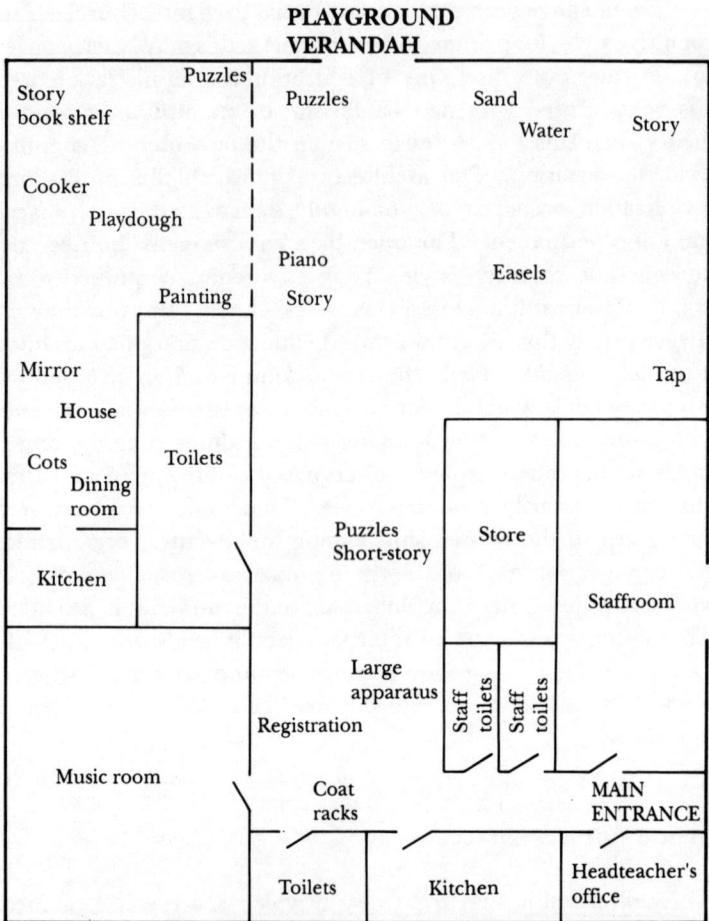

Figure 6.1 Ramsay: floor plan

Take, for example, the two headteachers and the ways in which they employed spatial means to mark the relationship with their respective staffs. Both had an office near the main entrance, opposite the staffroom. The office was the room furthest away from the activity areas. At Castleton (as stated earlier), neither the nursery teacher nor the headteacher took their coffee break with

PLAYGROUND
VERANDAH

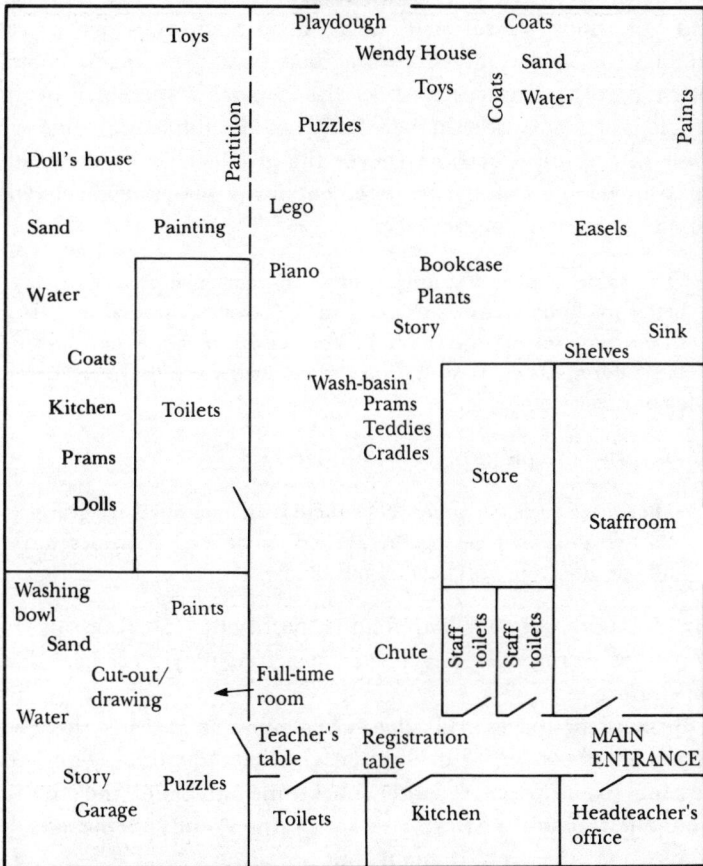

Figure 6.2 Castleton: floor plan

the nursery nurses. This, according to the headteacher, permitted the office telephone and doorbell to be manned during break. (The unintended effect of this was to separate the nursery nurses from the nursery teacher and headteacher.) Consider a second example. Castleton had a 'full-time' room. The children in this room were usually those from the poorest families, most of whom took 'free meals'. No such separate provision for the 'full-time' children obtained at Ramsay: they were fully integrated with the 'morning' and 'afternoon' children. (The room at Ramsay which corresponded to Castleton's 'full-time room' was the 'music room', although other activities were also provided therein.) In the previous year at Castleton there had been 'discipline problems with some of the full-time boys (never the girls). That produced the three areas.' This spatial arrangement, it was said, had affected the quality of play in the nursery:

> 'The value of play was lost in the open-plan. The quality of play is better in closed areas — so many of the boys ran around. . . . I can sit down more with the children. You can cover more; you can study the children easier. Last year they were out of sight; they played us off against each other.'

At Ramsay the philosophy was different:

> 'There used to be two areas. Now there is an integrated age group and full-time and part-time together. When you divided, it divides the staff and you don't get to know all the children.'

Finally, both schools had folding partitions. At Ramsay, the partitions were never closed; at Castleton, they were closed for snack-time.

Because the spaces at Castleton were more demarcated there was an attendant concern with children who 'left their area'. This 'trespassing' usually occurred after snack-time and before the children went out to play. In Miss Yates's area, the Wendy House was, by convention, the girls' domain, but not always so:

> *Extract from notes*: Alex is restrained from banging pieces of playdough together. Some boys are now in the Wendy House. George shouts through the Wendy House window at Donna, who complains to Miss Yates. She comes across: 'Boys, leave the girls to play in the Wendy House.' Another nursery nurse enters the area in pursuit of George. He immediately sits down. She picks him up and lifts him to her area.
>
> The noise level is high now. The Wendy House and its contents are in disarray. A boy runs around, chased by Michelle, who says, 'Stop running!' Donna skips around the area and eventually sits down with Michelle to look at a book. Miss Yates stands up, hands on hips, a little

concerned. Meanwhile Kelly, George, Donna and Vicki are flinging things round in the Wendy House. Nearby a boy is making a play-dough mask, then a necklace. Some nursery nurses are moving equipment outside. John swirls his playdough rope around his head. Donna, a large girl for her age, tries to butt into the group at the sand tray, but is pushed away. Calm is eventually restored: 'The morning boys are all big and pally . . . you've just got to quieten them down . . . split them up.' The children put on their coats, choose a partner and line up to go outside: 'When the bell rings it means we've got to come in.'

The demarcation of space at Castleton appeared to turn more on matters of social control. The open architecture was 'closed' by a separate room for the full-timers and by 'areas' for part-timers. As stated earlier, this arrangement was not made at Ramsay, despite its identical architecture. Whereas at Castleton spatial provision may have reflected the headteacher's priority for safety and social order, at Ramsay it may have had more to do with Mrs Smith's concern to protect the children and to preserve their innocence:

> 'There's no point in fighting this building. . . . They're not supposed to run around, but if they're enjoying themselves, it's a shame to stop them.'

In short, the two working-class nursery schools showed considerable differences in their internal spatial arrangements, with Castleton being the more clearly demarcated.

Let us turn to the middle-class nursery, Fieldhouse (Figure 6.3). It was a purpose-built unit within the complex of a primary school, being physically separate from it. Within Fieldhouse, there was no quest for symmetry of the type suggested below in Mrs Smith's staffroom at Ramsay. The notice below was placed there by the college staff who trained the nursery nurses, not by Mrs Smith (the notice was intended for the trainee nursery nurses who were on placement at Ramsay):

Artwork Display on Walls

1. Ensure all papers used are cut straight and right-angled — using the blue trimmer;
2. Write the child's name lightly in pencil;
3. Back onto thicker paper, leaving a margin of approximately 1.5 cm at three sides and a margin of 2 cm at the bottom of the picture — having decided which way up the picture goes, write the child's

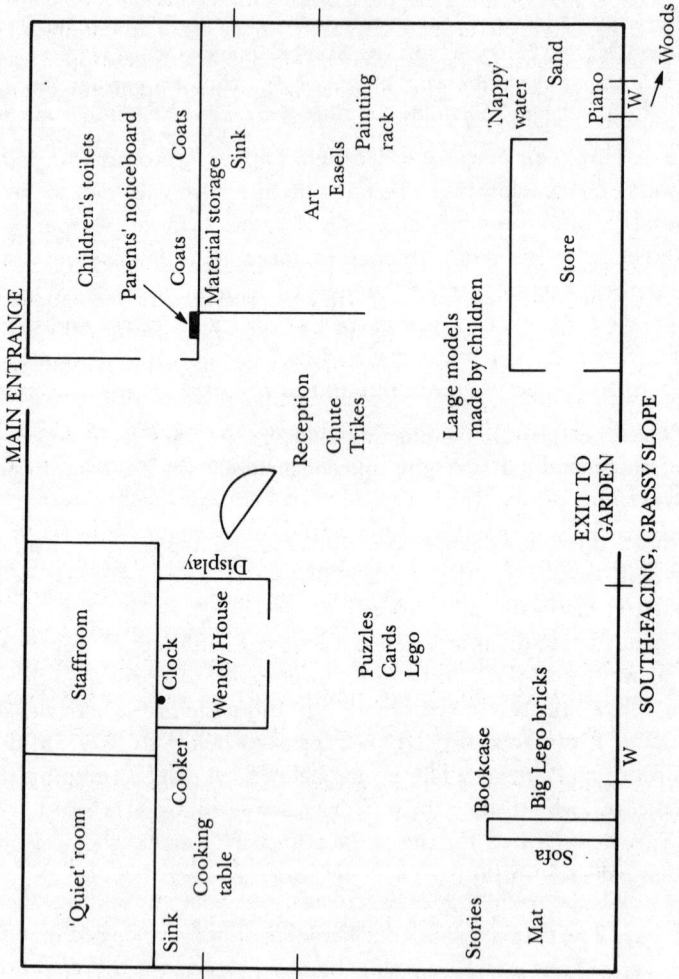

Figure 6.3 Fieldhouse: floor plan

name at the top left corner, using infant lettering;

4. Link a series of pictures: if each picture contains a few colours, then use the same colour backing-paper for all pictures (remembering that if the pictures are monotone, then different coloured backing paper may be used, but must blend with the background above).

5. Panel where pictures are displayed: (a) the space around the set of pictures must be the same at the top and both sides (top sides in a straight line) (b) The interior spaces (round the pictures) must all be equal to each other.

6. Only pin up collage pictures if the material used is well stuck and not liable to fall off.

7. Pin picture in position then check it.

Miss Foot and her colleagues had little time for carefully mounted work arranged to the nearest centimetre, and no time for templates and other objects produced to the exact specification of the staff. She was not interested in mass-production and the symmetrical arrangement of objects, be they items of furniture or of the children's art; and nor was she interested in having the children line up formally when moving from inside the nursery to the playground, as occurred at Castleton. Fieldhouse, therefore, was the least fixed in its spatial allocations. Moreover, Miss Foot at Fieldhouse and her staff would have been concerned about any perceived *surfeit* of space. Areas in Fieldhouse were not publicly labelled as 'art' room or 'play' room: 'They're divided in our minds', said Miss Foot. Walls, ceilings and windows were all festooned with the children's non-templated work. Miss Foot's maxim was, 'No templates please'. One visitor remarked:

'This would give me a nervous breakdown . . . all these mobiles hanging around!'

The mobiles at Fieldhouse were not of a fixed pattern and they were slung just above the children's heads, not near the ceiling out of the way. The displays were neither backed nor suspended in strict symmetry. The children could be seen mounting a step-ladder (held by the teacher) in order to pin up their own work. Normally this work was not a separate, free-standing piece, but would be part of a combined effort according to a theme, more of which later. The windows of the staffroom and outside walls were used as the surface for coloured finger paintings, giving a stained-glass appearance.

83

For example, one part of a wall had green reeds and rushes painted beneath the window, and the reeds were extended onto the window itself. Later in the year, this part of the wall had been converted to a 'greenhouse', with a translucent sheet enclosing both a window pane and a table top beneath it on which plants grew. While Miss Foot was interested in appearance, she wanted a 'guddle' (a mess, or muddle). Beneath the surface symbolism of this guddle, however, was a deeper coherence and integration of spaces and endeavours. Even the cloakroom contained displays of the children's work, made (appropriately) from the cardboard cylinders of toilet rolls. Whereas some might want to preserve an orderly and permanent environment, Miss Foot sought a continual transformation of the aesthetics and form of her nursery. At Fieldhouse, therefore, there was freedom within a structure, a desire to transform the given architecture and materials of the nursery, not to adhere to them.

Mobility between internal and external nursery areas

To what extent was there a strong spatial demarcation between the internal, walled spaces within a nursery and its external boundaries? Of all the nurseries, Ramsay was the least likely to send the children outside to play. The headteacher reported that the playground was dangerous. There was, for example, a large mound through which a rough concrete cylinder protruded (later removed, though present at the time of my visits). Deep pot-holes marked the stony surface, and these collected water in wet weather. Broken bottles were often thrown into the playground, and it was not unusual to find Evostik tubes and bags containing the remnants of glue. All of this was a far cry from the Scottish Education Department's preference that there should be:

> grass, tree trunks, plots of earth, trees, shrubs, winding paths, mounds and hillocks as well as paved areas and a covered and sheltered verandah.[9]

This concern with fresh air, gardens and shelters harks back to the McMillan sisters' pioneering work in nursery provision for the poor. Then, only open shelters had been provided to accommodate children when it rained. In cold and foggy weather, fires and braziers were lit, but it was very much a matter of fresh air being seen as related to good health. All this was in marked difference to the grassy glades at Fieldhouse. At Ramsay I observed an occasion when all the children and staff made a 'train' which 'choo-chooooed' round the playground and back into the school. (The impetus for this was a child telling a nursery nurse about the train on which she had travelled to visit her grandmother. Other children heard the conversation, and, quite spontaneously, a game developed which included the teacher and two nursery nurses.) But this excursion had been a rarity. One substitute nursery nurse at Ramsay remarked:

> 'They don't go out much here . . . I think they need to get out . . . maybe ten minutes to let off steam.'

No doubt the permanent staff would have agreed, provided that the playground had been a safe haven for children, which it was not, through no fault of the staff. All of the windows at Ramsay had net curtains drawn across them; only the Perspex roof dome remained without cover. While Mrs Smith at Ramsay had a fairly open space policy *within* the school building, she operated a relatively *closed* policy when it came to 'letting the children out', perhaps because the playground was bereft of the shrubbery and grass which she wanted. Indeed, the very large number of house-plants in the school may have been a compensation: that is, she brought 'nature in' rather than take the children out to play within the rather drab, concrete confines of the playground, itself surrounded by the decaying housing scheme which fed her nursery. Making the local environment relevant to the nursery curriculum may have been appropriate at Fieldhouse, but at Ramsay the two were kept apart. In this, she was perhaps protecting the children again.

Mrs Chalmers at the other working-class nursery, Castleton, took a different view. Weather permitting, the children normally went outside to play after snack-time. Castleton was by far the most crowded nursery, and taking the children outside was regarded as an essential form of catharsis. The play, however, was very structured and centred around the following pieces of apparatus: fifteen tricycles and pedal cars; mats; see-saw; bricks; sand; chute and steps. Aside from those on tricycles, the children's play was closely set within the apparatus provided, all of which had to be moved by the staff. Some of them complained that the physical effort in doing so was arduous. In other words, once outside in the playground, the children moved around defined 'play' areas, and these spaces were no less fixed than the 'areas' within the building itself.

At Fieldhouse, arrangements differed again. Because the school had been built on a former farm there remained a large grassy garden with mature trees. There was a place to dig holes and to plant flowers. But Fieldhouse departed from the practice in the other nurseries by allowing 'inside' activities to 'flow' outside. For example, children could use the tricycles both inside and outside the building, although space inside was very limited indeed; Nippy the guinea-pig was caged inside the school, but was 'exercised' in the 'woods'; there were tadpoles and three goldfish; plants and flowers were constantly brought into the building to embellish the rich visual spectacle already created by murals and models.

In summary, 'classroom'/'garden' exchanges varied: at Ramsay they rarely existed, but, through plants, nature was 'brought in'; at Castleton, exchanges were frequent, but structured, possibly to allow the children some degree of cathartic release, but within the strict bounds of safety standards; and at Fieldhouse, whose 'garden' facilities were excellent, the highest level of exchange was noted both within and between the internal and external spaces of the nursery.

School and locale

The degree of exclusion between nursery and community also varied. Most open to parental inclusion were the two working-class nurseries: the times when parents could come and collect their children were very flexible, especially so at Ramsay. Parents could enter the 'areas' at will, and there were notices welcoming them to join in the nursery activities. At Ramsay, 'mums', 'dads' and 'grannies' were notified that they could always 'come in for a cuppa'. Reflecting on the parents, Mrs Smith said of them:

> 'A great group of mums last year. . . . Every Wednesday they repaired books, sewed, did jigsaw puzzles, helped on the trips. The dads are always in . . . to repair things . . . and the grannies too.'

The staff at Castleton 'saw the mums every day' and relations between staff and parents seemed to be very friendly. Some parents
were thought to be less than competent:

> 'Some of them think things [such as toilet training and talking] just
> happen. There is no stimulation . . . they're just left in prams. They
> are really behind, even at three.'

Nevertheless, this degree of competence was more of a level that
the staff would expect of themselves as parents, and there was no
suggestion that the parents were culpable; indeed, they were said
to be making the best of what their circumstances would allow. The
parents were more than welcome, and particularly so when a new
child entered the nursery. Take the case of Anna at Castleton. For
the first two days, Anna stayed only for an hour. On the first day,
her mother, who was holding a baby, remained in the staffroom,
where she was encouraged to make herself tea. Back in the area,
Anna was introduced:

> 'This is a new girl, Anna . . . would you like to play with her?' (A
> student takes her by the hand to join some girls in the Wendy House.)

A little after ten o'clock Anna's mother returned to the area where
Anna had sat down for juice-time. The nursery nurse publicly
informed the mother that Anna had helped to tidy up. Turning to
Anna, she continued:

> 'Did you enjoy yourself? Are you coming back tomorrow? . . . Bye,
> bye Anna: You come back and see us tomorrow and your painting will
> be dry!'

The following morning Anna was again welcomed:

> 'Can you take your coat off?' (Her mother unbuttons it and takes it
> off. She then goes to the story corner with her baby, where she watches
> and waits for Anna.)

This openness towards the parents may have been an unintended
form of family therapy: that is, the staff could set an example to
the parents about how to treat their children. No such instruction
was deemed necessary at Fieldhouse. Parents brought their children to the registration desk at the entrance to the nursery unit.
Apart from helping their children in the cloakroom (where notices

to parents were posted), the presence of parents was very rare. Only at the outset of the school year would they be invited to stay in the staffroom if their children were having difficulty being assimilated into the nursery.

The registration procedure at Ramsay was a little more protracted. A parent selected the relevant yellow, green, red or blue badge which was to be pinned to the child (though some parents were less than assiduous in this respect):

> *Mrs Smith*: It's a bit formal but gives the parent or me a chance to talk about anything.

Most vigilant was Mrs Chalmers at Castleton. For example, at departure time she always checked that the children were being removed by only those adults who were legally supposed to take them. These measures, therefore, protected the children from abduction. Other measures protected the building from theft and vandalism, such as the aforementioned fence around the school. Thus, the greater numbers of children under the headteacher's charge at both Castleton and Ramsay, together with the perceived greater likelihood of vandalism and child abduction, may have caused the staff to exercise considerably more stringent procedures during 'going-home' time.

The Wendy House — no hiding place

Erving Goffman in his classic study of asylums provides a useful categorization of space in institutions.[10] Some spaces are 'off-limits', such as the staffroom; some spaces are under 'surveillance' to varying degrees. If surveillance is low, then the space may become 'open', beyond the scrutiny of officialdom, thereby providing an area in a nursery where an 'underlife' may flourish undetected. This area in a nursery allows the children to 'be themselves'.

When a child enters a school for the first time, he or she is expected to become a pupil, not a child. Ironically, if the pupil misbehaves he may be told off for being 'childish'. As adults, we move in and out of formal organizations, and as we do so we are expected to behave in the manner prescribed. This normally requires us to 're-invent' ourselves as we play our repertoire of roles. Within organizations, the space where we can be ourselves is very limited. Even when 'the boss' is out, his or her 'spirit' may pervade our workplace. What is distinctive about nursery schools is that they often claim to be places where children can be themselves. But this claim is rarely realized because there are very few spaces where the eyes of adults cannot intrude on the children's activities, particularly in open-plan nursery schools. Nevertheless, most nurseries may provide a zone of low surveillance. Often it is called the Wendy House. (The 'Wendy House' name comes from the small house built around Wendy in J. M. Barrie's *Peter Pan*, published in 1904.)

What counted as the 'Wendy House' (or 'House') varied, both in location and in form. The floor plans of the three nurseries show a variety of locations: Ramsay's is tucked away in a corner, largely beyond the gaze of staff: it is also relatively large in area. (Later in the research it was moved to a high-surveillance position opposite the door of the toilets.) Castleton's Wendy House was virtually at the centre of the school and, had it not been for its 'walls', would have been easily monitored. At Fieldhouse the 'House' had relatively high walls and a narrow entrance.

The contents also varied, but tended to include cooking, dining and dressing-up facilities. The Wendy House at Castleton had curtains and a narrow 'door'. Within it was a kitchen table, chairs and ironing board, together with cutlery and crockery. At Ramsay, a screen separated the 'lounge' from the 'kitchen'. The lounge comprised two sofas, four chairs, a coffee table, a telephone, four prams, two cradles, dolls, a collection of handbags, a dress-up rack and a full-length mirror. The kitchen contained a table, three chairs, kitchen units, plates, a plant, and a dustpan and brush. (Towards the end of my visits, most of this was moved near to the toilets, and a 'hospital' was added.) In general, if the children were in the Wendy House they were more likely to be corrected for 'being themselves'. Furthermore, the girls, not the boys, saw the Wendy House as their domain, particularly at Castleton, and they defended it vigorously, as these extracts reveal:

Two girls, Donna and Kay, seem to control the Wendy House. Stephen enters the Wendy House where the girls were setting out plates. He takes one and puts it on his head. They watch him. It falls off. 'Go away,' says Kay. He does but returns and sits down quietly in a chair.

On another day, Natalie's presence is not wanted:

She enters the house holding two handbags and a doll. She talks to Kay and Vikki. Kay then cuddles Rae. Natalie sits down on a dining table chair, but Kay tries to pull away the chair, unsuccessfully. Donna also fails to dislodge Natalie. Rae then snatches one of Natalie's handbags, and Kay tries to take her doll, again unsuccessfully. Kay then kicks Donna; Vikki leaves the Wendy House but returns shortly after. Meanwhile, Kay begins to 'iron' Donna's trousers while she is wearing them. Natalie takes the plates out of the basin.

Usually Miss Yates supported the girls if the boys were 'bothering' them. On one occasion, Gary shouted at Donna through the window. Donna complained.

Miss Yates: Boys! Leave the girls to play in the Wendy House.

The boys had sometimes 'been themselves' in too unruly a fashion in the Wendy House:

Nursery nurse: (to boys who had made Lego guns): There's no 'A Team'. We don't allow guns!

Boy: Why no 'A Team'?

Nursery nurse: 'Cos it gets out of hand in the Wendy House. The last 'A Team' smashed up the Wendy House. Go and make something really interesting [with the Lego].

Although the Wendy House at Castleton offered some 'invisibility' to the children, it was noteworthy that, by virtue of its contents, it offered limited facilities for play. These may have reinforced the domesticity of girls and caused the boys to be more 'creative' in their usage of those provisions. I did not see boys or girls being told off in the house area at Ramsay, but this was possibly the consequence of the low degree of supervision which it attracted. At Fieldhouse, the 'House' was little used compared to elsewhere, and, when it was, it tended to attract the girls:

(A nursery nurse removes a dress from the rack.) 'Isn't it beautiful?'

(She places it against a girl, who puts it on.) 'Isn't she lovely?! Turn round. Oh, it's lovely! Now what else do the girlies wear!'

Apart from its sartorial significance, this extract is also interesting in that here the nursery nurse has entered the Wendy House. Soon after, so did I, hoping to observe, but the nursery nurse soon left, as did all the children, leaving me alone. The relatively low occupancy rate of the House at Fieldhouse may, in addition to its easily surveyed central position, have been related to the greater maturity of the children there. They may have felt less in need of acting like children, so to say, in a private space than their counterparts elsewhere.

SUMMARY

In this and the previous chapter the focus has been on the ways in which time and space were managed in the three nursery settings. No claims were made that these arrangements necessarily produced effects on the psychology of the children. What has been argued is that to varying degrees the managerial regime of the nursery accords with the bureaucratic organizational forms which typify the wider society. This adherence to the bureaucratic form may be thought to be unremarkable. In a sense, that is the point: the bureaucratization of the child in institutional settings is now deemed to be the natural thing to do. The 'nature' of the child is now that which we have *constructed it to be*. Children may tacitly acquire frameworks which, to different degrees, will render them 'naturally' disposed towards bureaucratic forms.

But not all of these nursery schools were of a piece in the purity of their bureaucracy, and it is this variation which is of interest and which requires explanation. It would be too deterministic an argument to say that the nursery passively reflected the predominant institutional forms beyond it. The members of a nursery will *interpret* those forms. The interpretations which have so far emerged in the three nurseries are as follows.

At Fieldhouse there was evidence of what Bernstein has referred to as the 'invisible' pedagogy (discussed in Chapter 2). This comes close to Rousseau's preferred pedagogy of 'discovery learning'. Its managerial equivalent in work-settings would be a 'loose bureaucracy'.[11] There was, therefore, an interesting coincidence at Fieldhouse: that is, there was a coincidence between the idealism of child-centred educational philosophy and the emerging human relations managerial practice in service sector/professional work-settings. The idealism was embodied in Miss Foot; the 'soft', human relations bureaucracy was embodied in the parents who followed professional careers. The two were mutually reinforcing.

In Chapter 2, I discussed the assertion that Scottish infant education has a reputation for greater formality than that in England.[12] Even the Scottish 'Primary Memorandum', which anticipated many of the child-centred sentiments of the Plowden Report of 1967, becomes trapped in the contradiction between behaviourism and child-centredness. Of the latter, it states:

> The primary school child has a natural curiosity and a desire to learn which make him capable of seriously and deliberately pursuing his own education on lines of his own choice.[13]

Of the former:

> The teacher should produce a programme of work for her class for perhaps a month ahead, setting out the topics to be covered, the skills that are to be learned, and the activities that are to be undertaken.[14]

> The school routine, the organisation of the classroom, the teachers' methods, the content of the programme of work, the conduct of school meals and other social occasions . . . all help to *condition the attitudes and behaviour of the pupils* [emphasis added].[15]

The *superficial* similarity between the regimes at Ramsay and Fieldhouse may be explained thus: Mrs Smith, ever mindful of the dire circumstances in which many of her children lived, sought to protect them and their innocence. Education would be tantamount to improving speech and hygiene — those very practices which, at Fieldhouse, were assumed to be present in the children. Mrs Smith gave them freedom and little pressure. They were children: children should be happy, and her nursery should make them so. Castleton appeared to typify the very contradiction between formality and friendliness, freedom and structure, which the 'Primary Memorandum' so clearly exemplifies. There was a sense of dilemma, even unease. The staff at Castleton may have been caught between child-centred, nursery educational philosophy and the formalism which may have marked the wider culture.[16]

NOTES AND REFERENCES

1. Sommer, R. *Personal Space*. Englewood Cliffs, NJ: Prentice-Hall, 1969, p. 8.
2. Hall, E. T. *Beyond Culture*. New York: Doubleday.
3. Ibid., p. 15.
4. Bentham, J. *Panopticon; or The Inspector's House* (reprinted in *The Works of Jeremy Bentham*, Volume 4). New York: Russell & Russell, Letter 1, 1791, reprinted 1962.
5. Oldham, G. R. and Brass, D. J. 'Employee reactions to an open-plan office: a naturally occurring quasi-experiment'. *Administrative Science Quarterly*, **24** (2), 267–84, 1979; Hedge, A. 'The open-plan office; a systematic investigation of employee reaction to their work environment'. *Environment and Behaviour*, **14** (5), 519–42, 1982.
6. Sommer, op. cit. (1); David, T. 'Environmental literacy'. *School Review*, **82**, 687–705, 1974; Hamilton, D. *In Search of Structure*. Sevenoaks: Hodder & Stoughton for SCRE, 1977.
7. Propst, R. 'Human needs and working places'. *School Review*, **82**, 609–16, 1974; Sommer, op cit. (1), p. 99.
8. Neill, S. R. St. J. 'Pre-school design and child behaviour'. *Journal of Child Psychology and Psychiatry*, **23** (1), 316, 1982.
9. Scottish Education Department. *Before Five*. Edinburgh: HMSO, 1971, p. 38.
10. Goffman, E. *Asylum: Essays on the Social Situation of Mental Patients and Other Inmates*. Chicago: Aldine.
11. Bidwell, C. E. 'The school as a formal organization'. In March, J. G. (ed.) *A Handbook of Organizations*. New York: Rand McNally, 1965.
12. Roberts, A. F. B. 'Scotland and infant education in the nineteenth century'. *Scottish Educational Studies*, **4** (1), 39–45, 1972.
13. Scottish Education Department. *Primary Education in Scotland*. Edinburgh: HMSO, 1965, p. 12.
14. Ibid., p. 39.
15. Ibid., p. 90.
16. Humes, W. *The Leadership Class in Scottish Education*. Edinburgh: John Donald, 1986.

CHAPTER 7
Making the Connections

The main organizational forms in modern industrial society are variants of Weber's pure bureaucracy. Constant exposure to these forms may tacitly structure our common sense in ways that are conducive to these variants. This is not to say that everyone is a clear-cut case of 'organization man', but nevertheless the majority may be able to act, *without reflection*, in bureaucracies, be they for the purpose of leisure or livelihood. Occasionally some may find themselves enmeshed in 'red tape' — that is, they may find it irksome that one bureaucrat is unable, or unwilling, to go beyond his or her remit in order to expedite their concerns. (Of course, on another occasion, one may find that two officials whose roles are formally defined as different do in fact duplicate the *same* task, thereby prompting the complaint that 'the left hand doesn't know what the right hand is doing'.)

A central feature of bureaucracies, therefore, is that they structure their endeavours in such a way that the formal goal is fragmented, itemized and ordered sequentially so that the successful performance of the component goals will bring about the overall purpose. This means, however, that those who perform the specific and narrow component tasks will not have an overview of the organization. To use Berger *et al.*'s term, their view will be 'componential', not holistic.[1] Item analysis, not thematic analysis, will be their concern. Reality will be regarded as a collection of 'parts', devoid of a matrix or structure to integrate them.

This componential style of thought is not part of our innate psychology. It has already been argued that 'cottage' industrialists and agrarian workers of the pre-factory age did not adapt readily, or naturally, to the temporal and spatial restrictions of factory-based entrepreneurial capitalism. Initially they were cajoled into doing so; latterly they were exposed to the persuasions and precepts

94

of the Protestant ethic and the elementary school. It was there that the bureaucratic cognitive style was increasingly and tacitly rendered as 'natural', as common sense.[2]

In nursery education we have the beginnings of this production of a 'nature' amenable to the forms of bureaucracy. The analysis so far has considered the interrelated concepts of time and space in nursery education. In passing, the structuring of the children's activities has been alluded to. These arrangements are now considered in more detail. The analysis will take the following form: first, in the three nursery schools, are the children's activities defined as specific, discrete, unrelated tasks, or as being integrated into an overall theme? Second, are the children expected to undertake these activities in concert with, or independently of, others? Third, is it possible to locate the three nursery schools within a framework which incorporates these two previous considerations, and, if so, are these allocations explicable sociologically?

In a bureaucracy roles are defined *for*, not by, the individual. Tasks are clear-cut and are related interdependently. But it is the *tasks* which interrelate so as to produce the overall desired effect — those who perform them may not see their place or purpose in the scheme of things: they 'play their part', 'do their bit', so to say. This division of labour, of tasks, was evident in each of the three nursery schools. That is, there was a rota of activities which individual staff members followed. The activities were usually music, baking, singing, drama, games, painting, playdough, puzzles, large or small construction toys, sand tray, water table, dressing up, drawing, Wendy House, slide and snack. The degree of attention which staff gave to these activities varied. For example, the sand tray and water table would be left to the children unless they were seen to be doing something 'silly', like flicking sand in each other's faces, pouring water over each other, or making guns out of Lego. The children's 'silly sanctuary' tended to be the Wendy House. It was there that the children could play, be creative, be childish, be imaginative. The concern here, however, is not with the degree of supervision which attached to a given activity, but with the ways in which the activities themselves interrelated, and, by implication, the ways in which the children acted socially.

Table 7.1 The structure of the children's activities

	Thematic?			Collaborative?			Supervised?		
	R	C	F	R	C	F	R	C	F
Group A:									
Music	X	X	Y	Y	Y	Y	Y	Y	Y
Baking	X	X	Y	Y	Y	Y	Y	Y	Y
Painting	X	X	Y	X	X	Y	X	X	Y
Woodwork	B	B	B	B	B	B	B	B	B
Group B:									
House	X	X	X	Y	Y	N	X	X	X
Water	X	X	B	Y	Y	B	Y	X	B
Sand	X	X	X	Y	Y	Y	Y	X	X
Chute	X	X	X	X	X	X	Y	Y	X
Group C:									
Jigsaw	X	X	X	S	S	S	X	X	X
Reading	X	X	X	X	X	X	X	X	X
Construction	X	X	Y	S	S	Y	X	X	Y
Group D:									
Story	X	X	X	X	X	X	Y	Y	Y
Games	X	X	X	Y	Y	Y	Y	Y	Y
Drama	B	B	X	B	B	Y	B	B	Y
Riding	B	X	X	B	X	X	B	Y	X

Notes: R = Ramsay; C = Castleton; F = Fieldhouse.
Y = Yes; S = Sometimes. X = No; B = Activity not observed.
Collaboration for group A: At Fieldhouse, the staff initiated the collaborative endeavour across these activities. Elsewhere, collaboration meant that staff initiated collaboration within an activity. Collaboration for group B activities meant child-initiated collaboration.

The structure of activities is summarized in matrix form in Table 7.1 for each school in a manner that indicates (i) if the activity was normally linked to a general theme; (ii) if it was normally undertaken collaboratively with other children; and (iii) if it was normally undertaken under the close supervision of staff.

A number of points should be made to facilitate the interpretation of the matrix. If an activity is 'thematic' it is *related* to other activities. (The example of how 'music' related to other activities is discussed shortly.) If an activity is 'collaborative' it means that the children were jointly engaged in the activity. Children observed merely sitting together would not be considered to be acting in concert. That said, collaboration took two forms: teacher-defined collaboration; and child-initiated collaboration. Take the former: the group A activities (music, baking, snack, painting and woodwork) could be either collaborative *within* an activity (for example, everybody helped to bake a cake), or collaborative *across* activities (for example, that cake, in the shape of a bus, could be integrated into a song or drama about a bus). In the latter category of collaboration, particularly in respect of the group B activities, it was the children, not the staff, who collaborated, often unsupervised. For the staff, this accorded more with their notion of 'play' or fantasy. In order to give some sense of the actual events beneath the classifications in the matrix, consider the case of music: its function, form and substance within the three nurseries.

During the colder months, at Castleton, music was sometimes in the form of a concert-type exercise. Its execution was highly organized: the children marched towards the designated 'concert' area, accompanied by their 'shaking' and 'banging' percussion instruments. There they sat, correctly, with straight backs and crossed legs, intent upon the instructions from the pianist, in the person of Miss Bond. Not all of the children held a musical instrument — those lacking one were encouraged to clap their hands, but not to stamp their feet. Here, therefore, was supervised and ritualized sound, in tune and in time, with the children in place, sitting on the floor at the feet of the staff. Time, space, sound and style were all set by the staff. In some sessions, the piano was replaced by an electronic musical synthesizer, controlled by the headteacher and the nursery teacher. None of this was associated with other endeavours in the nursery. Its purpose may have been to integrate the school socially, using music as the medium. One nursery nurse referred to it as a 'display'. At other times (though I did not observe them) the children were said, by the headteacher, 'to enjoy music and movement games or ring games'. When the weather became warmer, the incidence of music decreased proportional to an increase in outdoor play.

Fieldhouse, the middle-class nursery, was very different. It was there that music, painting, construction and baking were all of a piece. These activities were highly coordinated and thematic. If the theme was 'transport', the children baked biscuits with red, green and amber icing so as to resemble traffic lights; they painted murals of buses, cars, zebra crossings, roads and so on; they made low-slung mobiles of trucks; they had finger-painted a 'train' on the window; they built large models of vehicles out of boxes and wood, some of which they rode; at snack-time they talked about toy vehicles:

Nursery nurse: What have you got in your pocket . . . cars and buses? (The nursery nurse holds up a toy bus.)

Nursery nurse: Is it a special one? Is it one that goes to the airport? What about this? What colour is it? RED!!

Nursery nurse: How many wheels on it? FOUR!!

Nursery nurse: You *are* clever this morning! (The cake, in the shape of a bus, was then brought in.)

Nursery nurse: How many windows does it have? TWO!!

Nursery nurse: What did we use? Eggs . . . flour . . . apples . . . butter . . . sugar . . .

(After snack-time the children moved to the 'story mat' for singing.)

Nursery nurse: Let's think of a song about a bus:

The horn on the bus goes Beep, Beep, Beep *all day long*.
The wheels on the bus go round and round *all day long*!
The bells on the bus go tingalingaling *all day long*!
The mummies on the bus go CHATTER CHATTER CHATTER *all day long*!
The dads on the bus go NOD, NOD, NOD *all day long*!

Music at Fieldhouse, therefore, was not an end in itself, but a means to an end, namely the pursuit of a theme which was defined by the staff. Nor was it highly ritualized, to be played in an assembly of the whole school.

Ramsay, likewise, did not have 'concerts'. It did, however, have a 'music room', the same room which at Castleton was used as the 'full-time room'. Its use, however, was not confined to music: it also contained prams, puzzles and small construction toys. The intention at Ramsay was to stress music as a social activity *per se* and to define it as play. It was presented to the children as a game. That is, before the children chose (if they so wished) a percussion instrument, they all played 'musical bumps' whereby they skipped to the piano music, falling to the floor when the music ceased, eliminating the person who was last to fall. Not all of the children in the music room joined in: a few completed jigsaw puzzles. Then, after the musical bumps and the children's selection of instruments, a more formal approach ensued:

Mrs Laird: First of all: instruments down on your knees. You've got to bang on the drum or shake this. Susi, which do you want to do?
(Mrs Laird plays the piano. They all clap to the rhythm.)
Now pick up your instruments.

A few boys stand at the periphery, watching.

Mrs Laird: Now just sing it. Put the instruments on your knees. (They sing in unison, joined by some of the boys doing puzzles nearby. Finally they both sing and play their instruments to the tune of 'Pop Goes the Weasel'. After the song the nursery nurse then asks an onlooker, Brian, if he would like a drum, but he declines.)

Mrs Laird: You just want to sit and listen? OK.
(A new approach is then tried. Mrs Laird plays the piano accompanied only by the drums. The tambourines are introduced. In the next version, those playing bells, triangles and maracas are the accompanists. Finally everyone plays the song: 'If you're happy and you know it, clap your hands'.)

Thus although the children were not compelled to play, once they chose to do so they had to comply with the nursery nurse's arrangements.

Mrs Smith, Ramsay's headteacher, incorporated singing with snack-time, as had occurred at Fieldhouse, but it was not thematically linked to other activities. It was seen as fun and as giving the children comfort and confidence. I have already referred on p. 68 to Mrs Smith's patient and considerate attempts to help Craig 'perform' before the other children at snack-time. Here she helps Elizabeth:

> *Mrs Smith*: This time there'll be a girl: Elizabeth! We must be quiet for Elizabeth! (She puts her arm around her as she sings. All the children clap at the end.)
> After a girl we'll have a boy . . . Michael . . . What are you going to sing? 'Baa Baa Black Sheep'! (Michael performs, receives applause and a 'very good' comment from Mrs Smith.)

Miss Faulds also introduced snack-time music, but again it was unrelated to other activities. First the children were made ready for the performance:

> *Miss Faulds*: On your bottom . . . sit on your bottom!

The children proceed to sing a 'song about a hammer': Peter plays with a hammer: 'Biff, Bang, Bing'. The singing is accompanied by stamping of the feet on the floor, and smacking of the hands on their knees. Meanwhile, in another part of the nursery, 'Head, Shoulders, Knees and Toes' was being chanted.

Music aside, there were other indications of the thematic approach at Fieldhouse. The *café* theme, I was informed, had lasted 'for ages'. The children cooked and baked for it; they made a restaurant and uniforms; they comprised the 'staff', or, as a nursery nurse put it:

> 'One of them led you to your seat — frightfully posh — took orders.'

The *jungle* succeeded the *transport* theme. I was able to see the beginnings of the project take shape: in the art room a nursery nurse was helping the children to paint some large boxes. They were coloured with brown spots on a yellow background so as to resemble a giraffe. At the sand tray two boys were discussing elephants, not at the teacher's behest, but at their own instigation:

> (A boy 'flies' an elephant shape over the sand tray.) 'I've never seen an elephant that flies.'
> 'What do you call an elephant that flies?'
> 'Dumbo!'
> 'A jumbo jet!!'

This reference to elephants and reality is reminiscent of Mehan's analysis of standardized language testing in the USA. In one example, he reported the children's responses to the question which required them to choose the animal that could fly. The options were: bird, elephant and dog. 'Bird' was the correct answer. Some of the children chose 'elephant', a wrong answer. When Mehan asked these first-grade children why they had chosen elephant, they told him about Dumbo, the elephant that flies in Walt Disney cartoons.[3]

After snack-time the children sang a song about 'Silas the Snake'. Earlier, children had painted concentric circles in different colours, and Miss Foot showed them how to cut the circles to make multi-coloured spirals: 'long, twisty snakes to go in the jungle'. Three days later the jungle display was complete. There were three child-sized animals (giraffe, tiger and elephant) made out of boxes, the elephant being strong enough to be ridden. These were set before a mural of snakes and other animals, none of which had been done with templates. In the adjoining room a 'sea display' was being put up. A blue background had been painted and the children were busy mounting their own 'fish' on it. Displays at Fieldhouse were of short duration as compared with those in the other nurseries.

Another activity common to most of the nursery schools was baking. Consider the ways in which the activity was provided at Castleton, Ramsay and Fieldhouse. Take Castleton: Mrs Jones sat at a table with ten children. She weighed the baking dough and then helped each child to break an egg into the mixing bowl. As each egg broke they all joined her in saying 'CRACK!' The ingredients were then added:

'Sugar, egg, flour . . . and what else? And what are we making? We'll have it tomorrow.'

Each child had a 'shot' at stirring the mix, and each 'had a lick' of the mix. That done, they all trooped off to the kitchen to see what would be done to the cake-mix. Here, therefore, is an example of collaboration *within* an activity, as directed by the nursery teacher. The following day the cake was eaten, and that was that.

At Fieldhouse, a cake had been made in the shape of a bus, thereby linking it to the transport theme. Later, at Eastertime, the children were baking 'nests' made of a mixture of chocolate and Rice Krispies, in which an egg or two was placed. All this was linked to a 'spring scene': a pond, some yellow paper chicks, hens, lambs — all models made by the children — with reeds on a backdrop, the reeds extending onto the window. A new 'spring' mural had been painted. Near the entrance was an asymmetrical display of individually made Easter baskets. The following day the children went outside to 'roll eggs', which they carried in their baskets. The nursery teacher, Miss Foot, wore her Easter bonnet in the nursery, but removed it when a parent came in. Later the children could go across to the infant school to see the chicks that were being hatched in the children's sand tray. (On another occasion at Fieldhouse I was reminded of the multiple realities which children hold: I had been sitting with the children at the puzzle table when a little girl demurely offered me a plate containing pieces of lime-green fudge. I took a piece, thanked her and put it in my mouth only to discover that it was playdough. I hesitated before telling her how good it tasted, after which she went about the nursery, offering the 'fudge'. No child made the mistake I had made. On another occasion at Fieldhouse, three children mixed real dough while two others mixed playdough on the same table.)

At Ramsay, fantasy-food, in the form of playdough, was frequently made and discussed:

Mrs Fletcher: Now what are you making here? Are you making something for my lunch? I don't want anything that's fattening. I'm on a diet . . . there's no sugar in it? (She 'tastes' it.) That's gorgeous, delicious cake!

Later a little boy appeared to be about to eat the 'food':

Mrs Fletcher: Yer no eatin' it Martin are yer?!!

Baking, therefore, was a discrete activity at both Castleton and Ramsay, unrelated to other activities, but nevertheless very much a social, collaborative endeavour under the guidance of the teacher.

All this has been concerned with collaboration of a kind whereby the nursery teacher/nurse helps the children work together at an activity which may (as at Fieldhouse) or may not (as elsewhere) be integrated with other activities. Other collaboration was observed, and it centred either on 'play', as in the Wendy House, or on helping one another to do a puzzle or to construct a toy. This form of child-initiated collaboration occurred in all nurseries. To illustrate this, fieldnotes from two mornings' observation of 'free play' at each nursery are summarized below.

Free play

Play is a central concept in early education. It is open to many definitions. In our discussion of Elias's concept of civility, we noted that the civilizing process is one which curtails the expression of the emotions and desires. It is to acquire a sense of shame. Education in its widest definition incorporates this acquisition, this moving beyond a state of unfettered emotionality. It is freedom within limits, not licence. In early education there is emphasis put on *freedom*, on the children *being themselves*, or being *natural*. But this must be weighed against the consideration that individual children are social as well as individual beings. To be social is to be aware of others, not only of oneself. So free expression must — if the child is to be educated — be set within what the social will allow. Consider Maria Montessori on a related theme:

> It would be much simpler to declare that an organism as yet immature, like that of a child, has remote affinities with mentalities less mature than our own, *like those of savages*. But even if we refrain from interfering with the belief of those who interpret childish mentality as a 'savage state', [. . .] education should help the child to overcome it; *it should not develop the savage state, nor keep the child therein* [emphasis added].[4]

This qualification of what freedom means is much discussed in the hallowed texts of early education. Take the Hadow Report:

> Freedom is essential; and freedom only becomes dangerous when there is nothing to absorb the child's restless activity and provide an outlet for this experimental spirit.[5]

Or Plowden:

> He works off aggression or compensates himself for lack of love by 'being' one or other of the people who impinge on his life.[6]

Or the Scottish Education Department:

Some children may find relief in acting out their emotional problems and they may learn about other people's reactions through the play situations.[7]

Much of this cathartic, therapeutic purpose of play develops, or repeats, Susan Isaacs's ideas in the 1920s:

If we watch such children at play, we shall see that their play is a safety valve for their hidden wishes and fears.[8]

Just as play may be thought of as giving vent to pent-up emotions, so too may it be thought of as being the medium of the child's expression of what adults would deem fantasy. Questions of what is real and what is not are, to some extent, questions which can only be resolved through the use of power. The world of objects has no intrinsic meaning: meanings are assigned to them. Children and adults face the same world of objects, and both can make sense of them. Multiple realities are evident, though we often find it difficult to come to terms with another person's way of seeing, or making sense of, the objective world. If that world-view is particularly at odds with our own (what we would call 'commonsense') view, then we may be tempted to regard it as silly, or abnormal, fantastic, unreal. Young children are very sophisticated interpreters of the objective world. For them, it is logical, but we self-styled rational thinkers often reduce it to the level of fantasy. In our more pompous moments we can liken the realities of some societies to that of children, and call them primitive, or underdeveloped. In short, the infant's reality must be developed in the direction of the 'real world', not the child's. Fantasy is allowable, but only as a step in the direction of the 'universe of fact':

Scope should still be afforded for 'make believe' in the children's play, but their fancy should not be over stimulated, and should be brought increasingly into contact with the universe of fact by encouraging them to follow their developing interests among real things. On the other hand it is most desirable that phantasy should be wholly ignored. . . .[9]

Let us return to 'free play' in the nurseries in the study. The setting is the 'full-time room' at Castleton on 24 September 1985. Mrs Turner and Miss Bond, both nursery nurses, were with sixteen children. The room door was open. Miss Bond sat at a table making playdough, discussing football with the boys. At another table Mrs Turner helped the children draw with felt-tip pens. Ryan wandered over to Mrs Turner, looking a little lost (his friend John had not yet arrived). The girls at the table made room for Ryan, but some of them left to join Moira at another table where she was playing with a construction toy. At 9.30 Keri arrived, to Mrs Turner's greeting of 'Morning, Keri'. Jennifer was walking about with a doll:

Mrs Turner: Are you needing a cuddle? Is she (the doll) needing a sleep?

Meanwhile Miss Bond continued to make the playdough:

'This is kneading.'

Stephen, wearing an earring in his left ear, was asked:

'Are you remembering to go to the toilet?'

Back in the full-time room, four boys were at the water table. Derek, who was in his second year in the full-time room, was saying 'quack, quack' and was making very authentic trumpet sounds with the water funnel. Mrs Turner: 'I say, Derek!' He continued. Mrs Turner: '*Derek*!' He stopped. At 9.30 four children (Ryan, Keri, Michelle and Moira) were doing puzzles. John was putting the components of a toy together by himself. Most of the girls who had been drawing with Mrs Turner had now switched to Miss Bond's playdough activity. At this point Mrs Chalmers, the headteacher, entered the room and stopped the errant Moira from going around telling everyone the colours of her toy. Mrs Chalmers crouched down, eye to eye with Moira. Moira immediately sat down. In another part of the room Mrs Turner and Ryan hugged each other. Meanwhile Mrs Chalmers tried to get Moira to sit with her and draw, much to Moira's pleasure. Mrs Turner, at 9.40, sat with Derek, John, Steve and Michael as they played with snap-on construction toys. Derek had made an octopus and proceeded to wave its tentacles about. Amanda approached Mrs Turner with her picture. 'It's a pipe', she said. 'A pipe,' replied Mrs Turner, 'What do you do with a pipe?' Amanda: 'Water goes through it!' Miss Bond, preparing slices of apple for juice-time, was given a playdough worm. Feigning surprise, she said: 'And here's a little worm wriggling into the apple!' Mrs Turner pointed to the binmen outside the room, gave Ryan yet another cuddle, and reminded the children that juice-time was imminent. Hazel was told to hurry up with her jigsaw, was helped to complete it and told she was a good girl. Ryan, in turn, was praised for his 'grumpy faced' picture, even though he himself had a 'smiling face'. It was then 'five minutes to juice-time'. Keri was to wash his hands, which he did, and Miss Bond helped him to 'halve the apple'. At 9.50 the children divided, half to Mrs Turner's table, half to Miss Bond's, and juice-time began. On other mornings before juice-time this same procedure repeated itself: that is, there were table activities which were supervised, such as painting and drawing, or games which helped the children learn geometrical shapes and colours; there were unsupervised table activities, such as puzzles; and there were non-table activities such as pram-pushing, doll-cuddling, water, construction and playing with toy cars. In this room the children received more cuddles than in any of the other nurseries. Aside from overtly selfish behaviour, the children in the full-time room were permitted to symbolize themselves as they wished. There was no physical aggression; there were lots of cuddly toys for the children to comfort. The children's freedom, however, was spatially limited to the room, even though they were permitted to transgress the limits of adult logic. There were no areas available to them beyond the surveillance of the two nursery nurses. They could not, for example, retire to the privacy of the Wendy House, a refuge open to those children outside the full-time room, in the 'areas'.

In the 'areas' (outside the 'full-time' room) at Castleton the observations were more difficult, not only visually but also aurally. On 15 October 1985, the activities in Miss Channing's and Mrs Michie's were as follows: making playdough; doing jigsaw puzzles; the Wendy House; the sand tray; the water table; Lego; reading corner. In the Wendy House were Hannah, Amy and Stephanie; at Lego were Craig, Christopher and Gary; playing with sand were Neil and Guy. Dawn began to cry, was picked up, offered juice, but declined it. (Later the headteacher told me that Dawn's mother had informed her that the child had been up for the previous two nights 'fiddling with the portable TV'. Mrs Chalmers had advised the mother to remove the television and to refrain from giving Dawn sweets before nursery school.) The sand tray was occupied by boys for much of the pre-juice-time period. The nursery teacher extracted Amy from the group to 'teach' her: 'Let's see what we've got in the box this morning'. George, whose reputation for misbehaviour was unsurpassed at Castleton, was reminded not to stray from Mrs Michie's area:

'The minute he disappears, send him back.'

As juice-time approached, some children used the Wendy House furniture for climbing purposes; George had indeed wandered out of his 'area' and was being walked back to it; Gary was reading; Neil, Paul, Christopher and Parvaz had taken over the Wendy House; Samantha, Jenny and Dawn were playing with construction toys; Stephen and Claire were cuddling each other; Paul had cornered all of the playdough and was resisting attempts by Karen and Claire to make him give it up; John started to throw the playdough; George screamed; Paul sported his playdough moustache; Jenny was recalled from the adjacent area. Juice-time was then announced, on time. The impression, therefore, of these pre-juice activities at Castleton was that they were to be chosen freely by the children, provided that they remained in their designated areas. Occasionally, a group of them would be taken out of the area to a table near the kitchen where the nursery teacher would help them with their numbers and colours. The part-time, 'morning children' in the areas had the opportunity for greater freedom of movement and expression than their full-time counterparts. They were less easily observed, particularly in the Wendy House, where fantasy was acted out, privately, before the other children. (I referred earlier to Kay ironing Donna's trousers while Donna was wearing them.) And beyond the Wendy House voices could be raised to levels much higher than in the confined acoustics of the full-time room. Nevertheless, the children were asked to remain in their own area, but this request was not enforced unless it produced behaviour beyond the limits of safe sociability. (The use of 'guns' and other 'weapons' was not allowed in any nursery; even the aggressive 'crashing' of toy cars was curbed. Aggression — even when ritualized — had to be diverted into more civilized 'activities'.) As in the other nurseries, freedom ended with juice-time.

At Ramsay the children were allowed 'free play' for most of the morning until eleven o'clock, apart from snack-time. Normally, the activities were much as they had been at Castleton, though there appeared to be fewer children. The 'full-time room' (as it was called at Castleton) was used by all. There were usually equal numbers at playdough, water table, cars/story mat, construction toys, painting, Wendy House, puzzles, the chute/trampoline mat and at music. Again, as at Castleton, the children's fastasies were allowed: for example, a nursery nurse was seen bathing a baby doll with real soap and water. There were very few group activities, aside from those musical and cooking activities already considered. Towards the end of the morning, at about eleven o'clock, the children would sometimes be seated for a story or game. *Hats for Sale* is an example:

> The children sit before an easel which has been covered in black cloth. Those children who are going home at 11.15 sit on the carpet at the front; those staying to lunch are on chairs at the back. Three houses are stuck onto the cloth. A man, the hat seller, is also attached. The nursery nurse then puts a red, white, blue and yellow hat on his head and asks the children to name the colour of each hat. She next produces a yellow, spoked-wheel shape. 'What's that?' she asks. 'A spider!' 'No,' she replies, 'It's the sun. Because the man is in the sun he needs shelter.' A tree is added to the picture so that he can sit in the shade. He falls asleep and some monkeys are added to the branches of the tree. They steal his hats and take them up the tree. On waking, the man stretches, and looks up and sees the monkeys above him with his hats. All the children say 'GIVE ME BACK MY HATS', and the monkeys say 'YA YA YA'. The monkeys throw down the hats. As each is thrown the man puts it on, and the children state its colour. At the end, a number of children are invited to take off a piece from the board, naming its colour as he or she does so.

The mornings at Ramsay were the most free of all the nurseries, with little direction or ritual to follow. The children were allowed 'to be themselves' as much as possible, save for the routines of snack-time. Collaboration was very much at the instigation of the children, not the staff. Themes centred about festivals or the circus, but the production of models, murals and plays was very limited when compared with Castleton. There, for example, one nursery nurse told me she had spent a morning cutting out templated 'black cat' shapes. In a later aside she said that the various festivals 'means hats for everyone — and masks too':

> (Sixty hats had been cut out like a production line.) 'You're not enjoy-
> ing it and the kids aren't. It loses the sense of fun.'

Mrs Chalmers later told me that templates were rarely used, the
exception to the rule being when party masks were being produced.
At Christmas time the nativity play at Castleton ran for two weeks
and was performed nine times before an audience of parents. (At
Fieldhouse there had been two performances, with two dress
rehearsals, one for the staff, the other for the children in the infant
school. The play was not regularly performed, nor was it required.)
The greater number of performances at Castleton turned on the
greater numbers of children in the school, of whom there were 140,
who were divided into nine groups, each of which invited friends
and parents to join in with the singing and to watch the children
in the 'Nativity Tableau'.

At middle-class Fieldhouse the 'free play' combined both themes
and individual choice, as these observations from a pre-snack-time
period suggest: two boys were at the sand tray, a girl played with
the doll's house, and six children were sponging green paint onto
the back of rolls of wall-paper, brought in by parents. Miss Foot,
the nursery teacher, helped them. Nearby, two girls played at the
water table. From the ceiling hung five large mobiles of trucks, all
different, which were residues of the transport theme. The walls
on the southwest corner of the nursery were bare, awaiting the
jungle theme mural. Next to the sponge-painters was the sand tray,
where four boys were 'baking':

> *Alex*: I'm going to make a lovely butter cake.
>
> *James*: I put in potato. (They all stir the same cake of sand.)
>
> *James*: Put sultanas on it.
>
> *Paul*: Put broccoli on it.
>
> *Andrew*: Put potatoes on it.

At 9.21 the boys left the sand tray. On the window of the room
the children had finger-painted a train of trucks. This merging
of wall-mounted paintings with window-based paintings was common at Fieldhouse, and is a further example of the ambiguous use
of space at the nursery. In the other room, French toast was being

made by five girls and a boy. Nearby three girls did puzzles, and four boys rode tricycles near the entrance to the school. The three sand-cake makers then entered the Wendy House. I was offered French toast which I was assured was not playdough. The boys watched a nursery nurse dress a little girl in the Wendy House and left immediately thereafter. A boy asked me if I knew how to make French toast. The question was overheard by a nursery nurse, and she peered over the wall of the Wendy House and said, 'So you can make some for your wife!' A girl walked about with a veil over her face. By 9.35 no one was riding the tricycles. Virtually all of the children had left the room where the painting had been going on, and most were seated: six sat with a nursery nurse doing puzzles; two boys were playing with Lego on the floor; I was sitting on some steps near the entrance. A boy asked 'Please can we have your steps?' On taking them he joined them with another set to make a 'car' for three children to drive, with sound effects. I had stood to watch this, but one boy, thinking that they had deprived me of my seat, said 'He'll fetch you a seat if you want.' As the boys sat on the 'car' they discussed 'The A Team'. Hannibal figured large in their analysis, and was defined as a 'goody', not one of the 'baddies'. The conclusion was: 'Goodies are goodies, and baddies are baddies.' By now three children were cooking and there were three girls pushing prams in the story area. At 9.43 only three children remained in the 'art' area. Meanwhile at the puzzle table a nursery nurse sat with Alan, arm round him, helping him. She clapped when he inserted a piece correctly. At the next table Roger and Moira were placing coloured pegs into a board. The pegs were in a jar, but a boy knocked it over with his toy locomotive, causing the contents to empty onto the floor. 'Oh no!', said Moira, 'you knocked all these down!' With neither complaint nor consternation the two 'peggers' collected the pegs, but the nursery nurse, Mrs Cathro, ordered the culprit to pick them up. At the cooking table:

Mrs Wright: If you spread toast when it's hot . . .

Moira: It burns your hand.

Mrs Wright: No, that's not it. It is something else . . .

Mrs Wright: What are these called?

Leslie: The crusts.

By 9.50 the noise level had increased: the trike-riders were ringing their bells with gusto; the 'peggers' were spilling the pegs at will. Miss Foot, at 9.56, ordered the children to tidy up. The French toast was duly set down on the tables ready for snack-time.

Much of this chapter has been concerned with 'non-directed' and 'directed' activities. The former were also termed 'free play' — 'free' in the sense that the children could choose from those activities on offer; 'play' in the sense that they were allowed to super-impose on those activities their own interpretations of them — in short, they expressed their imagination through the medium of sand, of water; and so on. They symbolized their fantasies in words and deeds, and provided these posed no threats to safety, they were given free rein. On the surface, the children constructed their own reality; they assigned their own meanings to the objects within their nursery school. But beneath the facade of 'free play' lay a formal structure not of the children's making. It was an arrangement of 'areas' and 'corners' which served to foster a particular aspect of the social and cognitive development of the child. The 'nature' of the child was being constructed, stage by stage, through his or her exposure to these separately arrayed activities. This, however, is to overstate: the child could choose this or that activity — he or she was not obliged to pass through all stages in the 'production process', nor in a particular sequence. But, for the most part, the activities for the children tended to be arranged separately, and were not intended to be seen relationally. In these endeavours the children acted alone or in groups, depending upon their perceived stage of sociability. On occasions they imposed their own relation-ship upon these discrete activities, as when they made a 'cake' out of sand, or used toy elephants (jungle theme) as aeroplanes (trans-port theme), or when they brought a teapot from the Wendy House and used it as a water funnel at the water table, or when they used a water funnel at the water table as a trumpet, or when they used spoon and pan as sword and shield. These reinterpretations of purpose were not intended consequences. Despite the disconnected form in which the staff presented the objects, some children were able to unite them into new symbolic arrangements in very logical ways, often to the surprise of staff whose own logic restricted them from thinking that these objects could 'fit' in this new way. The children, therefore, produced a new 'logic of the curriculum'. At 'tidy-up time', however, these creations were disconnected, tidied up, and stored in their 'proper place'.

The exception to this was Fieldhouse. In the previous chapter it was noted that ambiguity of spatial purpose was permitted. Neither areas nor children were rigidly labelled. At the level of activities, some — though not all — were structured in such a way as to reveal their complementarity to the children, usually through the 'media' of art, music and cooking. On this basis, therefore, there is an argument that Fieldhouse was the most structured of the nursery schools in that considerable planning was required which would allow the children to 'structure the structure', so to say. As Miss Foot put it, 'We are structured so they [the children] can be unstructured.'

Bureaucracy purports to be efficient and effective: that is, the goal should be achieved as planned, with economy of time and cost. This implies that quality control or monitoring has been undertaken. Each stage of the production process would be scrutinized and checked. Each component or activity would have been subjected to careful observation, the outcome duly recorded. Performance criteria would abound. In institutions such as nursery schools, which claim to allow free play, the pre-specification of outcomes, not their measurement, might seem superfluous. The current fad — the 'cult of efficiency' — in education requires a sophisticated and extensive bureaucratic means of measuring efficiency. In manufacturing organizations where the 'finished product' is readily recognizable and where the technology for treating the raw material is routine and agreed upon, the monitoring of performance is objectively possible. But where, as in 'people-processing' organizations (such as a nursery school), there are few agreed notions of technology and purpose, the use of objective, comparable indicators of efficiency is questionable. None the less, that most fashionable of monitoring instruments, the checklist, was evident, though not at Fieldhouse. The use of checklists was diagnostic, but they could equally be used later to inform the judgements of primary school teachers. Furthermore the checklist is yet another example of itemization, of componentiality, of the bureaucratic cognitive style. Consider the 'assessment' procedures at Castleton.

Quality control

At Castleton, the use of a very sophisticated assessment device, the Keele Pre-School Assessment Guide (KPAG), was used by the nursery teacher, not the nursery nurses.[10] The nursery nurses, however, sporadically maintained a checklist in their respective areas which noted the activities a child had engaged in during a given day.

The formal statement of assessment at Castleton occurs in the prospectus:

> There is continuous monitoring of a child's progress, and informal reporting of this between his parents and his staff. Where any significant difficulty is identified, this will be discussed with parents in the first instance so that the child can be given further help. Where a child with a particular problem has been enrolled at Nursery School, appropriate arrangements are made with the Head Teacher, and other agencies involved, to ensure that the parents are informed of their child's development.

At Castleton, the nursery teacher did not admit to 'assessing them, just monitoring them so that we know what to teach them'. As stated, to this effect, she used the KPAG. The nursery nurses also informally assessed the children according to a commonsense classification of 'development' which defined 'stages', namely:

> The *baby stage*: 'there is no evidence of toilet training; he can't speak; no cutlery skills; some are fed; little confidence in themselves — they just want to play'. (Mrs Turner said of her boys: 'Very immature, but they're really three.')
> The *solitary play* stage: 'they destroy, bash — watch George!'
> The *parallel stage*: 'they don't make things or build and play with one another until the parallel stage. They play by themselves; they are on-lookers. Then they play together', the *cooperative stage*: 'leaders and followers emerge; they play for a purpose, with confidence. It's a sort of voyage of discovery'.

The nursery teacher's expertise was questioned by the nursery nurses: 'She writes down who can do what. If she came to us we could tell her. There is no need to assess or compare.'

At Ramsay, the most working-class nursery, a less sophisticated checklist, reproduced in Appendix III, was used, but only at the

113

end of the child's nursery school 'career'. The comments on 'assessment' in the nursery's prospectus are virtually identical to those at Castleton. No written records were passed on to the infant mistress at the primary school, but individual children were discussed orally by Mrs Smith with the primary school staff. As stated in Chapter 3, Mrs Smith, unlike her counterpart at Castleton, was not a user of 'Keele'. Nevertheless, the staff argued that there were certain clues which indicated that a child had 'difficulties':

> They don't talk, just sit. One child was hyperactive and just jumped up and down all the time, bared his teeth, and would only play. He is now in a school for the maladjusted.

The least assiduous in the keeping of *formal* records was Fieldhouse, perhaps because most of the cognitive and social skills required in say, 'Keele', were assumed to be possessed by the child. The nursery's policy on assessment is stated formally as follows:

> A child's progress is continuously being monitored by the staff and this is reported to his parents in an informal way. Where any significant difficulty is identified, this will normally be discussed with the parents in the first instance so that the child can be given further help. Where a child with a particular problem has been enrolled at the nursery, appropriate arrangements are made with the Head Teacher and other agencies involved to ensure that the parents are informed of their child's development.

(Note that the procedures for helping a child suspected of having a 'significant difficulty' are nearly identical to those at Castleton, perhaps reflecting common advice given to all the nursery schools in the area.) Despite the lack of formal diagnostic assessment devices, the staff claimed to be able to identify a child who was in difficulty, or, at the other extreme, who was 'ready for school'. Of the former, the clue was, 'If they're just sitting, they're unhappy, insecure.' Of the latter, the signs were: '[the ability to] write names, numbers, recognize colours, pick out words in books, and boredom.' Miss Foot at Fieldhouse was afforded a high measure of professional autonomy by the headteacher of the adjoining primary school. This may have allowed her to proceed in a less formal manner in respect of assessment.

SUMMARY

I have argued that the dominant notion of childhood and pedagogy after the sixteenth century owes much to the writings of Locke and Hartley. The science of child development rests on the inductive scientific method, based on observation and classification. It culminates in Piagetian developmental psychology. *Monitoring* is a central strategy in the pedagogy of early education. Recall John Locke's assertion that:

> He that is about children should well study their natures and aptitudes and see by often trials what turn they easily take and what becomes them; observe what their native stock is, how it may be improved, and what it is fit for. . . .[11]

The 1967 Plowden Report calls for 'detailed observations' of individual children so that their stage of development can be discerned.[12] The Scottish Education Department echoes the foregoing:

> The child develops gradually through these experiences over a period of time. It is important that the teacher should be aware of the stage at which each child needs further stimulation. A simple record kept for each child helps the teacher to ensure that situations are provided at the right time to further a child's progression in play, language and development of understanding.[13]

The 'Keele' scheme and those related modes of assessment which use checklists are underpinned by the behaviourist strand in psychology. Within broad 'aims', 'outcomes' may be pre-specified, itemized and observed. This neatly avoids the difficult epistemological issue of whether or not it is logically possible to segment knowledge in this way. There are, too, issues which turn on how the nursery teacher or nurse interprets descriptors like 'timid', 'assured', 'exhibitionist' when applied to particular children in a particular school. Staff admitted that they might rate the same child differently against these criteria. And to this may be added the matter of how, say, a primary school teacher who receives that child's ratings might interpret them. Nevertheless, there *are* some outcomes which can be clearly specified and objectively observed, such as the ability of the child to button up his or her coat. But these examples are relatively few. Quite apart from the comprehensiveness of the lists and the uses to which they are put subsequently, the meanings which are attached to the terms are highly subjective, *but once the responses are symbolized in a non-verbal manner, either by number or by a tick, they appear to be more objective, scientific and impersonal than is the case.* They are seemingly standardized representations of inner mental states which purportedly allow for comparison, or transferability. Here behaviourism, developmental Piagetian psychology, bureaucracy, efficiency and childhood converge. (For an historical analysis of these 'normalizing technologies', see Foucault.[14]) The organizational arrangements of the nursery school may well become influenced by assessment checklists such as 'Keele', despite assertions to the contrary:

> Thirdly, the KPAG may provide an outline of and suggestions for activities in a nursery school setting. The suggested *items* may imply that certain *forms of activity* should be encouraged. Such implications appear to be inevitable in this form of guide. However, users are **not** encouraged to teach to the items and where these are at variance with the practice in a particular nursery they should be substituted. *Nevertheless, the listing of items may stimulate ideas about the pattern of nursery activities and furnish the user with a means of describing them* [emphasis in italics added].[15]

Recent developments in early education suggest that the tendency towards this kind of monitoring will increase. In the wake of the introduction of the National Curriculum in England and Wales, the government has convened the Under 5: Committee of Enquiry, whose first meeting was held on 25 May 1989, and whose remit is: 'To consider the quality of the educational experience which should be offered to 3- and 4-year-olds, with particular reference to context, continuity and progression in learning, having regard to the requirements of the National Curriculum and taking account of the Government's expenditure plan.' These increasing tendencies to focus on the measurement of outcomes are conceptually linked to compensatory programmes in the United States,[16] and have been regarded favourably by Strathclyde Region as a way ahead in Scotland.[17] They are symptoms of the extension of bureaucratic rationality into the world of the infant, and set aside the naturalness of the child, the freedom, the expression which was so much part of the Rousseau tradition. The issue, therefore, is more with the *form* that nursery school education takes than with the statements about its substance. It is this form which constitutes the hidden curriculum of the nursery school, and which to varying degrees accords with the dominant form of organization beyond the school, namely that of bureaucracy. There is thus an isomorphism, a similarity of form reminiscent of nested Russian dolls, between nursery school and society. The 'forms of activity', as Tyler noted above, are contained within 'areas' or 'corners', and the mode of assessment is again even more fragmented and itemized. All this, of course, may meet the response: 'So what? The children are being socialized into a broadly bureaucratic cognitive style in a society which itself is for the most part arranged bureaucratically. That is as it should be'. The difficulty with this response is that it does not square with the 'philosophical' rhetoric of child-centredness, with notions of 'play', 'freedom', 'the child as an individual', 'creativity', 'imagination', 'innocence'. At this point, the words of Rousseau are a timely reminder:

> Let him [the child] always think he is master while you are really master. There is no subjection so complete as that which preserves the forms of freedom; it is thus that the will itself is taken captive. Is this poor child, without knowledge, strength, or wisdom, entirely at your mercy? Are you not master of his whole environment so far as it affects him? Cannot you make of him what you please? . . . No doubt he ought only to do what he wants, but he ought to want to do nothing but what you want him to do.[18]

NOTES AND REFERENCES

1. Berger, P., Berger, B. and Kellner, H. *The Homeless Mind*. Harmondsworth: Penguin, 1973.
2. Vallance, E. 'Hiding the hidden curriculum'. *Curriculum Inquiry*, **38**, 5–21, 1973.
3. Mehan, H. 'Assessing children's school performance'. In Hammersley, M. and Woods, P. (eds) *The Process of Schooling: A Sociological Reader*. London: Routledge & Kegan Paul, 1976, p. 128.
4. Montessori, M. *The Advanced Montessori Method*. New York: Frederick A. Stokes, 1917.
5. Hadow Report. *Report of the Consultative Committee on Infant and Nursery Schools*. London: HMSO, 1933, p. 143.
6. Plowden Report. *Children and their Primary Schools*. London: HMSO, 1967, pp. 193–4.

7. Scottish Education Department. *Before Five*. Edinburgh: HMSO, 1971, p. 17.
8. Isaacs, S. *The Nursery World*. London: Butler & Tanner, 1929, p. 98.
9. Hadow Report, op. cit. (5), p. 83.
10. Tyler, S. *Keele Pre-school Assessment Guide* (Experimental Edition). Slough: NFER, 1980.
11. Locke, quoted in Rusk, R. and Scotland, J., *Doctrines of the Great Educators*. London: Macmillan, 1979, p. 93.
12. Plowden Report, op. cit. (6), p. 196.
13. Scottish Education Department, op. cit. (7).
14. Foucault, M. *Discipline and Punish: The Birth of the Prison*, translated by A. Sheridan. New York: Pantheon Books, 1977.
15. Tyler, S., op. cit. (10), pp. 3–4.
16. Makins, V. 'Curriculum cure-all?' *Times Educational Supplement Scotland*, **1091**, 25, 1987.
17. Strathclyde Regional Council. *Under Fives*. Glasgow: Strathclyde Regional Council, 1985, p. 67.
18. Rousseau, quoted in Darling, J. 'Progressive, traditional and radical: a re-alignment'. *Journal of Philosophy of Education*, **12**, 157–66, 1978.

CHAPTER 8
Breaking Them In

Modern capitalist societies are marked by social differentiation and social inequalities based on class, gender and ethnicity. They, like their socialist counterparts, are marked also by bureaucracy as the most prevalent organizational form. Since the 1930s, schools of management have increasingly softened the rigidities of the Weberian ideal type of bureaucracy by introducing a more humane element, and it is characterized by terms such as 'collaboration', 'participation' and 'choice', all of which comprise the so-called human relations theory of management. The mode of control 'exerted' by those managers who subscribe to the human relations approach is implicit: that is, organizations are structured so that individuals control themselves, by acting responsibly, rather than suffer more coercive ways of ensuring their compliance. There is, too, a greater concern with interpersonal relations: that is, rather than exchange memoranda, people are encouraged to interact on a face-to-face basis. There is less austerity and formality. There is more openness. It is this softer mode of organizational control which has traditionally typified the theory, if not the practice, of progressive primary education, and it is now beginning to operate (at the other end of compulsory education) in non-advanced further education, but for different reasons.[1] That is, whereas progressive primary education has long drawn upon a history of European educational philosophy dating back to Froebel and Rousseau, the impetus for the new learner-centred pedagogy in non-advanced further education appears to derive from the concern of employers that college-leavers should be used to acting responsibly, with little supervision, in the emerging service sector of the economy. In other words, the 'soft' bureaucracy of the college or school classroom should anticipate the human relations management regime of the workplace. Thus, whereas child-centredness in primary education has tended to be informed by a philosophical ideal, the new learner-centred pedagogy of further education has been informed by a managerial and economic concern. In both, an emphasis is placed on implicit modes of social control, rather than on overt, ritualistic, authoritarian forms.

All this has relevance to the earlier discussion of the sociology of Norbert Elias. With the 'dependence of all on all', there is a need for 'self-compulsion' and 'self-restraint'. Affects are suppressed by the self within the self. This is not to say that this moderation of impulses is total: it is not, but it is more prevalent in the modern age. Whereas hitherto the 'battle' was waged against others, now, when the forces of pacification are state-controlled, the focus of conflict shifts:

> But at the same time the battlefield is, in a sense, moved within. Part of the tensions and passions that were earlier directly released in the struggle of man and man must now be worked out within the human being.[2]

Nevertheless, this self-restraint is not found to equal degrees in all social strata:

> There are, of course, many unsolved problems raised by this vista. In the present context it may be enough to draw attention to the fact that by and large *the lower strata, the oppressed and poorer outsider groups at a given stage of development, tend to follow their drives and affects more directly and spontaneously, that their conduct is less strictly regulated than that of their respective upper strata* [emphasis added].[3]

The reason for the reduced level of affect suppression in these poorest groups is because they are threatened more by physical pain, or by 'annihilation by the sword, poverty or hunger'. This variation in the levels of self-control may, argues Elias, accord with social class and status group, though it must be stated that Elias is not specifically positing a class analysis of society from a Marxist perspective.

But to return to the nursery school, and to introduce again the question of social class: a number of studies have reported differences in the ways in which parents, particularly mothers, control their children in different social classes.[4] Working-class mothers report that they are more coercive than their middle-class counterparts. In the working-class home the naughty child is more likely to be blamed; in the middle-class home he is made to feel ashamed. In the working-class home, discipline is enforced; in the middle-class home, compliance is structured tacitly. In the nursery, there is, according to Bernstein, an accord between the mode of control in the 'new' middle-class home and that of the nursery school.[5]

While it is not the main purpose here to focus wholly on Bernstein's paper in which he analyses the social structuring of pedagogy in the nursery and infant school, there are, nevertheless, points of relevance for the data generated in the three nursery schools here and his analysis.[6] His central proposition is that the nursery school's pedagogy, which includes modes of control, will accord with the presumed mode of control which obtains in the homes of the 'new' professionals of the middle class. 'New' middle-class professionals derive their status from symbolic 'property', not physical property, unlike their Victorian predecessors. In the homes of these professionals, there will be much ado with negotiation and flexibility of roles, times and spaces. It is this 'managerial regime' which the new middle-class mother will seek in that nursery school to which she will send her child: a home from home, so to say. If this were so, it would be expected that Fieldhouse, the middle-class nursery, would hold to this 'invisible pedagogy'; and, on the other hand, the two working-class nurseries, Ramsay and Castleton, would be expected to be the more 'visible' and bureaucratic. Put differently, fewer explicit ways of enforcing discipline should be expected at Fieldhouse than at Ramsay and Castleton. These expectations were not wholly met. Consider, first, the ways in which social control was maintained at Fieldhouse.

'If men define situations as real, they are real in their consequences'.[7] This long-standing sociological maxim forms the basis of 'self-fulfilling prophecy' research in education.[8] With this in mind it is relevant to begin with the ways in which the staff of the respective nursery schools define their children and the expectations which they have of them. It should then be axiomatic that the ways in which they control the children should be in accordance with their expectations. For example, if children were defined as, say, innocent, then it would be illogical if they were thought to be culpable for misdemeanours, and to be admonished formally. Or, to take another example, if it were the expectation that nursery school children should be seen as embryonic pupils who should be made ready for the primary school, then their dispositions and demeanours would need to be moulded with this in mind, and their innocence and 'naturalness' cast to the wind.

At no time did I hear a direct admonition or 'angry question' towards a child at Fieldhouse. Furthermore, there were many activities allowed there which might have posed concerns for the child's safety. Climbing frame, trampoline, tricycles and other rideable toys were all arranged in fairly confined spaces. At Fieldhouse, the child's behaviour was usually corrected with the use of polite interruptions on the part of the staff. Mrs Merchant, for example:

'Excuse me. Someone is trying to tell me a story.'
'Excuse me. This is very fine sand and can scratch your eyes — it hurts.'

Praise, too, was seen as important: 'We praise them a lot.' Miss Lennox provides an example:

'What a lovely class. Let me see your happy faces.'

At Fieldhouse, what was noticeable was the virtual absence of direct admonitions. The 'freedom to control themselves' best summarized the practice there. When modes of control in the two working-class nurseries, Castleton and Ramsay, are considered, differences again occur, not only between the two schools, but within them. We begin with Ramsay.

Mrs Smith, the headteacher at Ramsay, advocated the preservation of the innocence and naturalness of the child. They were to be protected. It may be recalled that she wanted 'fairies, not ghosties' at Hallowe'en, and that the witch should be a nice one, not a nasty one. In the last chapter, when Mrs Smith was reported conducting her music session with the children, she was liberal with her cuddles and kindness to the children. Similarly, Mrs Laird, one of her nursery nurses, had not compelled the children to join in the playing of music if they had not wished to. Mrs Smith was equally unwilling to force the children to take part in drama:

'Boys, if you don't want to play [in the drama game] that's all right, but sit at the side.'

Aside from the ensuring of a degree of attention at snack-time, there were very few direct admonitions at Ramsay. The only one which I observed was Mrs Fletcher, a nursery teacher, who became a little 'annoyed' at Parvaz for painting a desk:

'Silly boy. Would you paint your mother's furniture like that?' (Parvaz then spilt the paint and was told that he needed to roll up his sleeves. He then discussed the face he had painted with Mrs Fletcher, who doubted its resemblance to a face. To help him, while speaking she pointed to her own face — nose, eyes, ears.) 'Have a look. It's a round head.' (Parvaz was then left to correct his face, and a short while later Mrs Fletcher returned to him, a little dismayed.) 'How do you manage to get the floor in such a mess?' (Ten minutes later, Parvaz was in the music room, doing a jigsaw puzzle. I could not establish whether he had been sent there.)

That aside, the children were treated with far more open affection at Ramsay than elsewhere. There were more dolls for the children and more cuddles given to them by the staff. When I asked why there were so many dolls, Mrs Fletcher seemed surprised that I thought there were:

'You provide what they like.'

An example of the tactile demonstration of affection concerns Jane. She was standing near the entrance to the toilets watching some children slide down the chute. There she stood, hugging her doll, for fifteen minutes. A little boy made a face at her, causing her to hold the doll tighter, for comfort. Mrs Jones walked by her, gently touching her cheek, thereby prompting a smile. The doll was then dropped, picked up, and its clothes adjusted. That done, Jane edged nearer the chute. Just as she appeared to be about to join in, Mrs Smith came by. Jane's face brightened. Mrs Smith kissed her on the head and told her that it was story time. Thereafter, Jane skipped to her story group.

At Castleton, there was a very wide range of techniques for controlling the children. Aside from snack-time and the rather ritualized music assemblies, discussed earlier, there were examples of physical exercise to get them ready.

Mrs Michie: Hands on your head, hands on your shoulders, hands on your knees.

More generally, there was the frequent removal of apparatus into the playground, and this was thought to have a beneficially cathartic effect. Direct commands were evident, though not often:

'JOHN. I haven't said you [can move]. Harriet and James, stand nicely like soldiers. Michael, you take George. Just walk nicely please.'

Diversions were in greater evidence. The boys were reminded that previous 'A Teams' had smashed up the Wendy House and therefore it would be better if they would make something really interesting. As at Ramsay, the use of cuddles, particularly in the 'full-time room', was common:

Mrs Turner: The children might become too attached in the full-time group. They get used to you giving them a cuddle and wrapping them up in a blanket!

Praise was also employed:

'You're a big girl now! When are you going to practise that [buttoning up a coat] for me?'

'Good girl! I think you're ready to go to school when you can do your coat like that.'

Finally there is the matter of the ways in which boys and girls were perceived.

'Boys! Leave the girls to play in the Wendy House.'

'That's it, Lorna. Show the boys how to do it!'

No statistical comparison was made of either the frequency or the type of controls which staff used on boys and girls respectively. At Castleton boys appeared to receive more correction of their actions, and this observation was supported by comments from staff:

(At Castleton): 'Boys are more immature — it's just the biology of the thing.'

'Some rogues last year created mayhem, all boys. You never get girls like that.'

(At Fieldhouse): 'Girls are little smarties in general. They're so clever. And some of them are so capable.'

These comments imply that, particularly at Castleton, the gender role of boys had ill prepared them for the institutional form of the nursery. There was 'no rough and tumble' for either sex, and while at Castleton there was much playground activity, it was highly structured and supervised, reportedly for reasons of safety.

In a general sense we have been concerned with the pedagogical relationship between nursery school staff and child. The nature of this relationship turns on the conceptual framework which a teacher or nursery nurse brings to her professional setting. She (for it tends to be virtually the preserve of women) views the child through an interpretative scheme which is itself generated within the society of which she is a part. To a considerable extent the *nature* of the child is a *product* of both this scheme and the interactions with the child which are a consequence of it.[9] In other words, the development of psychological theory — and here we are dealing very much with developmental psychology — may fruitfully be viewed historically and sociologically: historically because from this perspective it becomes plain that the nature of the child varies; and sociologically because, at a given point in history, the social structure may have consequences for what counts as 'the nature of the child'. For example, does 'boyhood' have different meanings in working-class and middle-class environments? Is the 'nature' of the female gender in white, inner-city society different from that in Asian, Muslim, inner-city society in Britain?

In this chapter, our central concern has been with modes of social control in the nursery school. To some extent, our earlier analyses of time and space dealt with the same concern. But whereas these earlier analyses were focused mainly on how spatial and temporal arrangements *tacitly* controlled the child, in this chapter we have sought to consider more obvious, overt forms of control of a tactile or spoken nature. Now it may be argued that nursery education is not in the business of control. That would obviate the need for play, preventing the sensations from being given free rein. There must be spontaneity; there must be nothing of rules and regulations. Of Emile, Rousseau said:

> He does not know the meaning of habit, routine, and custom; what he did yesterday has no control over what he is doing today; he follows no rule, submits to no authority; copies no patterns, and only acts or speaks as he pleases.[10]

It was this free, romantic view of childhood which Mrs Smith and Mrs Turner seemed to find attractive:

> *Mrs Turner*: I don't think we should interfere too much with the children's play. We should learn to stand back and let them come to you. . . . Children should have more freedom to be a bit more adventurous. Give them a measure of danger to live with. But that is not advocating less vigilance.

But their advocacy of this rather romantic and sentimental (in the sense that it assumes the affects and sentiments of the children should be *expressed*, not *suppressed*) view of the child may not only have turned on their philosophy of education, but also on a sympathy for the child whose domestic plight was to be pitied. (Mrs Turner, it may be recalled, was in charge of the 'full-time room' at Castleton wherein the vast majority of the children took 'free meals'.) In this compassionate endeavour, Mrs Smith and Mrs Turner both shared one of the causes of the esteemed Scottish pioneer of nursery education, Margaret McMillan, reports of whose work near the turn of the century in the slums of Bradford are seminal reading for nursery educationists.

This historical residue of romanticism which was incorporated in Mrs Smith's and Mrs Turner's educational ideology must also be placed against a set of social influences which brought the ideals of rationality, bureaucracy and behaviourism to bear on both their professional practice and their views of the social expectations of nursery education. For it is rationality and bureaucracy which suffuse such educational practices as timetables (snack-time, story time; and so on); groups and areas (often colour-coded); checklists of achievement, of registers, of name-tags, of registration ('clocking-in'); and monitoring of affective performance so that they can be seen to fall within the 'norm'. These quantifications of the mind, of behaviour, and these formalizations of space, time and demeanour along rational and bureaucratic lines are all manifestations of the bureaucratic cognitive styles of the staff themselves. They are, for most, commonsense and civilized behaviour. They require the suppression of impulses, feelings and spontaneous behaviour. In *relative* terms, the professional practices of Mrs Chalmers (at Castleton) accorded more with these manifestations, though her professed ideology also referred to the romanticism propounded by Mrs Smith and Mrs Turner. But herein lies the nursery teacher's dilemma: the cultural forces which impinge on her are typical of the bureaucratic society in which she lives, *and for which she may feel her children should be made ready, in however limited a way*; on the other hand, her charges are, after all, children who are to be permitted the freedom of play. Put another way, nursery educators, in trying to produce a strategy which reconciles this dilemma, must ask, 'What will be the form of the informal?' That is, what *organizational form* should a nursery school have so that it will best provide an *informal* atmosphere wherein play, freedom and bureaucracy can seemingly be accommodated?

A similar question had not been answered successfully in the late 1960s. The Bergers have pointed to the mismatch between 'permissive' middle-class child-rearing and the bureaucratic form in the wider society.[11] This discontinuity between primary and secondary socialization, they argued, unsituated young people, thereby prompting them to construct a 'counter-culture'. Since that time, formal bureaucracies beyond the primary school have increasingly 'softened', along the lines suggested by human relations management theorists. Thus it is that we heard much of 'collaboration', 'choice' and 'partnership' in education in the early 1980s, all of which have that liberal, democratic ring which was so often heard, albeit more loudly, in the late 1960s. But surrounding all this is also the clarion call for efficiency and the bureaucratic minutiae associated with curriculum modules, item-banks, profiles and appraisal. In other words, in the late 1980s, we have aspects of both progressivism and bureaucratic rationality co-existing in education, but perhaps not merging. In order to effect that merger, considerable managerial acumen is required. It was only at Fieldhouse nursery school that this delicate balance seemed to prevail.

NOTES AND REFERENCES

1. Hartley, D. 'The convergence of learner-centred pedagogy in primary and further education in Scotland: 1965–1985'. *British Journal of Educational Studies*, **35** (2), 115–28, 1987.
2. Elias, N. *The Civilizing Process*. Volume 2, *State Formation and Civilization*, translated by E. Jeffcott. Oxford: Basil Blackwell, 1982, p. 241. (Originally published in 1939).
3. Ibid., p. 251.
4. Newson, J. and Newson, E. *Four Years Old in an Urban Community*. London: Allen & Unwin, 1968; and Wadsworth, M. E. J. 'Social-class and generation differences in pre-school education'. *British Journal of Sociology*, **32** (4), 560–82, 1981.
5. Bernstein, B. 'Class and pedagogies: visible and invisible' (1975). In Bernstein, B. *Class, Codes and Control*, Volume III. 2nd edition. London: Routledge & Kegan Paul, 1977.
6. Ibid.
7. Thomas, W. I. *The Child in America*. New York: Knopf, 1928.
8. Rosenthal, R. and Jacobson, L. *Pygmalion in the Classroom*. New York: Holt, Rinehart & Winston, 1968.
9. Ingleby, D. 'The psychology of child psychology'. In Richards, M. P. M. (ed.) *The Integration of a Child into a Social World*. London: Cambridge University Press, 1974; Shotter, J. and Gregory, S. 'On first gaining the idea of oneself as a person'. In Harre, R. (ed.) *Life Sentences*. London: Routledge & Kegan Paul, 1977; Spiecker, B. 'The pedagogical relationship'. *Oxford Review of Education*, **10** (2), 203–9, 1984; and Walkerdine, V. 'Developmental psychology and the child-centred pedagogy: the insertion of Piaget into early education'. In Henriques, J., Holloway, W., Urwin, C., Venn, C. and Walkerdine, V. (eds) *Changing the Subject: Psychology, Social Regulation and Subjectivity*. London: Methuen, 1984.
10. Rousseau, J.-J. *Emile*, translated by B. Foxley. London: Dent, 1974, p. 125. (Originally published 1762.)
11. Berger, P. L. and Berger, B. 'The blueing of America'. In Berger, P. (ed.) *Readings in Sociology*. New York: Basic Books, 1974.

CHAPTER 9
Lacking the Piece of Paper

Weber foresaw that as bureaucracy burgeoned so also would there be a proliferation of the professions. It is the age of the expert. In order to legitimate their professional status, the holders of such positions require credentials which purport to certify their technical competence. The logical extension of this is that there is a direct and positive relationship between credential and competence. Credentials, however, imply that those who lack them cannot perform as well as those who hold them: there is no place, therefore, for the gifted amateur. Credentials can serve as exclusionary devices: that is, those who hold them can claim to exclude from their ranks those who lack them, even though the latter may be technically competent. Thus credentials have a *status*-conferring power.[1]

In addition to the exclusionary power of the credential, other devices can be employed by a profession in order to maximize its status, power and privilege. It may, for example, develop a jargon, or 'shop-talk', which to the outsider may be difficult to understand. This exclusivity may be enhanced if that jargon can claim to be founded on scientific principles and research, rather than on mere appeals to magic or tradition. To this we may add what is ironically a non-scientifically based device, namely the ritual. It is ironic because professionality, specialism and credentials are all marks of modernity, of a scientific society wherein natural and social phenomena are explained rationally. Ritual, however, harks back to a pre-scientific era, one when faith and magic were sufficient explanations of these phenomena. And yet ritual is retained to enhance the professional's status in the modern, scientific age. Finally, the more a profession can keep at bay the prying eyes of the public, the more its mystique can be preserved from criticism. Here, therefore, one is dealing with a spatial or geographical exclusion, rather than one based on credential, jargon and ritual.

In the nursery schools at issue here, there was a three-tier professional structure: the headteacher of a nursery school; the nursery teacher; the nursery nurse. The category of nursery teacher may be divided into those designated as teacher-in-charge of a nursery *unit* attached to a primary school, and those nursery teachers under the authority of a headteacher of a nursery *school*. Those above nursery nurse status normally undergo a three-year training period in a college of education; nursery nurses normally train for two years in a college of further education. The former register with Scotland's General Teaching Council (GTC); the latter do not. The former belong to one of the teaching unions; the latter belong to NALGO (the National Association of Local Government Officers). The nursery teacher can aspire to a headship; the nursery nurse cannot progress. And, finally, the highest salary paid to the latter is approximately equal to the lowest salary paid to the former. The justification of all these differences allegedly turns on credentials and duties: the nursery teacher *teaches*; the nursery nurse *nurses*. The former's remit attends to the mind; the latter's to the body. These two complementary mind–body endeavours combine to serve 'the whole child'. The highest degree of status differentiation obtained in the nursery which tended towards a more bureaucratic approach, namely Castleton. Within a school, the two complementary roles of teacher and nurse may not mesh in the manner prescribed. Rivalries and resentments may emerge, thereby constituting what Hoyle and Ball have called the 'micro-politics' of the school.[2]

Historically, nurseries were staffed by certificated nursery teachers and assistants, or 'helpers', who were trained in the school. Their role was similar to that of today's nursery nurse. In 1950, the Scottish Education Department required helpers to be young (16 to 20), healthy, energetic and of equable temperament, besides being well-spoken and of sound education. Because pay and discretion were low, the job was not regarded as a career, and was not supposed to be undertaken after the age of twenty-one.[3] Plowden called for a career which suited older women, and for a reduction of the two-year Nursery Nurse Examination Board (NNEB) course to one year, a procedure not adopted in Scotland. The Scottish Education Department subsequently recommended that nursery nurses might proceed to follow full teacher training.[4]

By the late 1980s, the definition and provision of nursery education were in a state of flux in Scotland. State-funded nursery education is not a statutory requirement, and the control of nursery (or,
to use the now-preferred term, 'pre-five provision') education
is being contested by regional departments of social work and
education. In Strathclyde Region, which is in the van of this
change, concern was voiced that in the deprived areas there was
little provision in the school holidays for the children. An enquiry
commissioned by the Region noted research that saw few differences between the work of the nursery nurse and that of the nursery
teacher. It recommended that new community nurseries be introduced wherein all staff would be on the same conditions of service,
and be known as 'pre-five workers'. Only one member would be
a teacher. Not surprisingly, nursery teachers have taken issue with
this attempt by a social work department to erode their professionality and status.[5] The matter raises many questions about
what counts as childhood and early education, but it seems clear
that we are dealing here with nurseries which are in deprived areas,
and the social work lobby is legitimating its encroachment on
welfare criteria, not cognitive ones. In some ways, the status
contest in nursery education between teacher and nursery nurse is
analogous to that between teachers and teacher aides (as defined
in the 1967 Plowden Report). There is, however, an important
difference: nursery nurses tend to outnumber the nursery teachers
in the larger nursery schools, and teachers resort (perhaps subconsciously) to devices for minimizing the power of the nursery nurses.
If, in deprived areas, the philosophy of early education is one
of caring, of protection, of retaining the child's innocence, then
nursery *nurses* can claim to have more of the required skills to deal
with this. If, on the other hand, a cognitive ethos emerges, perhaps
in response to the demands of parents, then nursery teachers
can claim the upper hand. The term 'nursery' (caring) 'school'
(cognitive) itself captures the dilemma, one which is resolved by
the term 'pre-five provision'. Some of these trends suggest themselves in the nurseries at issue here.

There are those in educational circles who posit a relationship between the age of the children taught and the attendant status
of the professional who teaches them. On that basis, those who
occupy positions in primary, secondary and further or higher

education may regard nursery education as 'not really education', and thereby afford relatively low professional status to nursery school staff. Mrs Chalmers, for example, recalled a reaction to her decision to enter nursery teaching: 'Aren't you teaching any more?' But *within* nursery schools, further status differentiation may obtain. In part, as stated earlier, this is based on credentials, of which the nursery teachers have more, and in part it is based on salary. At Castleton, Mrs Chalmers clearly took the view that her school should, if possible, prepare children for primary school: to stimulate them and prepare them for primary school in a caring, 'family' context. She appeared to want to help her children to compete for credentials when they entered compulsory education. In short, she tried to balance a caring philosophy with a merito-cratic one. It was to this that she seemed committed. As she stated: 'I'm never satisfied!' In her quest for satisfaction, she may have prevailed too much on her nursery nurses, one of whom commented:

> 'She wants perfection. Perfection doesn't matter to me, you or the children. She expects too much.'

This may have been an extreme interpretation, but another nursery nurse remarked upon Mrs Chalmers' vigilance:

> 'Mrs Chalmers comes out and spots something right away, even though you've told them not to do it!'

At Castleton, staff meetings were said to be rare, and the discussion of school matters had, by agreement, long been excluded from coffee breaks. (When I began the study, I had not been aware of this. As part of my research, I would often chat to staff about 'school matters' in their coffee break, thinking that this would enable me to clarify my observations. On some occasions, the staff were a little late in returning to their 'areas', thereby allegedly causing an adverse effect on the children's play. By implication, I may have been seen to have been interfering in the school's routine.)

> 'Many years ago we agreed not to use coffee breaks to discuss school matters.'

That said, Mrs Chalmers stated that she fully supported the expression of strongly held views. Privately, too, she was full of very high praise for her staff, though she agreed that it was not always publicly expressed.

Power is always in balance. It is negotiable. Although a headteacher holds formal authority over her staff, her power over them is never complete. As mentioned, Mrs Chalmers asserted that she fully supported the expression of strongly held views. Mrs Turner, in particular, appeared to lead an ideological group which called into question Mrs Chalmers' concern with safety and cognitive matters. A former member of staff at Castleton recalled that Mrs Chalmers was 'very safety conscious'. To this, Mrs Chalmers replied:

> 'People say I'm more cautious than the parents, but they don't have more than ten children.'

But central to Mrs Turner's concern was that Mrs Chalmers would not 'let them [the children] be themselves'. All this disagreement, however, was more latent than manifest. More publicly and widely aired by the nursery nurses at Castleton were their views on the so-called distinctions between 'teaching' and 'nursing', and their unequal status. The nursery nurses' position was clear:

> 'We are the first step away from mummy. Sometimes they call you mum or granny. Nursery nurses think of the whole child, not just the mental aspect of the child.'

They claimed that their duties embraced and went beyond those of the newly arrived nursery teacher, Mrs Bailie, and often were undertaken in more difficult conditions. Whereas, for example, Mrs Bailie could 'withdraw' a group to 'teach' them, the nursery nurses could not:

> 'The nursery teachers take out the children from the area because of the noise. We have to put up with the noise.'

The only differences appeared in the nursery teacher's attention to 'basic' cognitive skills and to assessment. To all intents and purposes these two duties were of a piece: that is she 'tested' (assessed) them on the (cognitive) 'basics'. But, said Miss Yates, a nursery nurse:

'They're [the teachers] not doing anything different with the children. We tell them! She writes down who can do what. If she came to us, we could tell her.'

And although the nursery teacher had 'the bit of paper', the nurses were not bereft of teaching ability:

'We have a different method of getting it out of them.'

None of this was aired in the presence of either Mrs Bailie or Mrs Chalmers, for they took their coffee apart from the nursery nurses, and no differences were seen to be expressed. Some years previously, when staffing levels had been more generous, the nursery teacher and the headteacher had shared the nursery nurse coffee breaks. At the time of the research, both the headteacher and the nursery teacher

'supervise in the play rooms during nursery nurse staff coffee breaks and continue to take responsibility for answering the telephone and door.'

But the nursery nurses' lot was not made easier by what some regarded as a total lack of career opportunities. For example, Mrs Turner remarked that there was no promotional system in nursery nursing. She wanted an intermediate position between nursery nurse and nursery teacher, along the lines which operated elsewhere, as reported by Miss Yates:

'In Drummond there is a career structure for nursery nurses: a senior nurse assistant and a junior assistant. And nursery nurses are moved after five years to keep them fresh.'

Mrs Chalmers set much store in attending to matters of administration, and her nursery nurses may not have appreciated the amount that she needed to do. These tasks were assiduously defined and classified. (The lists below also indicate Mrs Chalmers' interpretation of the administrative aspect of her role.)

SPECIFIC DUTIES RETAINED BY HEAD TEACHER

1. Initial interview — child's name entered on waiting list; discussion of practical details with parent; tour of school with parent and child.

2. Second interview with parent and child — admission form filled in by Head Teacher and signed by parent; more detailed discussion with parent; tour of the school with parent and child.

3. Supervision of Nursery Nurse Students — writing confidential reports for NNEB; attending co-ordinating panel meetings.

4. Supervision of training of Student Teachers sent by College of Education; writing of confidential reports at end of Teaching Practice. Discussion of progress of these students with College of Education Lecturers.

5. Keeping childen's reports of any deviations from normal in physical, mental and emotional aspects.

6. Write references for past and present members of staff who are seeking other positions.

7. Arrange (accompany when possible) visits to other Nursery and Infant Schools.

8. Discuss policy of school with visiting head teachers and other members of staff from other Nursery and Infant Schools.

9. Hold frequent formal and informal meetings with staff — in-service training team teaching in open-plan situation. Arrange medical appointments for children with school MOH, notify parents. Remain free at time of MOH visit to receive parents and withdraw child from playroom.

10. Invite small groups of parents to the school to discuss work of the school, answer queries and see each mother individually to have a two way talk about her child.

11. Liaison with secondary schools — HT may wish to send pupils to undertake some form of service for the children.

12. Make contact with Children's Home in the area and with Community Centre.

13. Take time to talk to Health Visitor.

14. Supervise and write report about Child Care Student.

15. Try to ensure that parents remember to keep appointments made with Dental Officer.

16. Twice weekly either issue library books a.m. and p.m. or supervise area of member of staff who is undertaking this task.

17. Answer telephone when possible.

18. Write log book.

19. Keep day to day record of school fund income and expenditure.

20. Assist probationer teachers, mature nursery nurses, students, or nursery nurse students.

135

21. Leave time for visits of (1) School Medical Officer, (2) School Dental Officer, (3) Health visitor students, (4) Pre-nursing students, (5) Interested members of the professions and the general public.

DELEGATED SECRETARIAL DUTIES

(It should be stressed that at the time of the research there was *no* secretary. Mrs Chalmers also informed me that there had been in excess of 1,000 incoming telephone calls per year over a three-year period.)

Weekly
1. Bank School Fund money on Monday.
2. Cash cleaners' wage cheque, make up wages — Friday.
3. Staff absence — folder and forms.
4. Enter petty cash — stamps, etc.
5. File all circulars and correspondence.
6. Write and despatch cleaners' work sheets.
7. Write and despatch work order forms.
8. Write and despatch workmen's time sheets.
9. Transfer children's absences from Reception Desk register to 'Daily Register'.
10. For all admissions/departures, enter/remove child's name from: Reception Desk register, Blue daily register (office), Name badge, Dymo name — coat peg, Medical card, Library card, Dental list, Milk group lists — language development, Art folder.
11. Type information circulars for parents.
12. Check accounts for requisition, supplies and despatch.
13. Mend library books.

Monthly
1. Milk form — write and despatch.
2. Monthly return (a) children's absences Form A1 Primary (b) Staff Form ST (NS).
3. Check medical supplies and order as required.

4. Check cleaning materials and supplies (paper towels, toilet rolls) and order as required.
5. File reports in area folders.
6. Type children's names for group lists.

Annually or biennially
1. Type requisition.
2. Type (triplicate) inventory for each area and cupboard.
3. Cover and label all library books.
4. Stamp all small apparatus, books and forms.
5. Make library folders.
6. Make art folders.

This formal expression of the headteacher's role at Castleton is highly explicit, and its degree of categorization and detail squares well with the structure of training given in a nearby college which trained nursery nurses, in so far as the college's statement of the curriculum and assessment is concerned. To elaborate: when trainees are on placement in a nursery, they are assessed according to checklists, one for each course module and its nested learning outcomes, both of which are numbered. At a deeper nested level are the objectives which contain the observational categories for monitoring the trainee's progress. As a trainee meets the criteria, the objective is checked off by a tick, dated, authorized and, if necessary, commented upon. The procedure has all the hallmarks of quality control in a factory. And just as the trainee is monitored, so too is the child. The segmentation of the nursery nurse's professional knowledge into modules and objectives — and the itemized checklisting of its acquisition — constitutes a hidden curriculum which exemplifies the bureaucratic cognitive style. This, however, represents the college-based ideal, not what occurs necessarily in nursery schools. What is interesting about this bureaucratic structuring of knowledge and assessment for the trainee is that she (for it tends to be a woman) must then go and *not* act bureaucratically and didactically towards the children. Children, they are told, are individuals, not amenable to standardized treatment. Put succinctly, these nursery nurse trainees are bureaucratically told to be not bureaucratic.

Consider this further. These trainees are located in non-advanced further education, which in Scotland was rationalized after the 1983 Action Plan.[6] That is, all non-advanced further education courses were collated, then divided into modules, each with its own performance criteria. Given that further education has had a traditionally close relationship to manufacturing technology, it is not surprising that it should adopt some of the managerial practices associated with it. If, on the other hand, the training of nursery teachers is considered, it occurs in colleges of education, where the hidden curriculum might be said to be less formal than in further education. The products of these sites of professional socialization meet in the nursery, where accommodations have to be made between them. All this is itself set in the context of the nursery's locality and society, both of which set limits on the professional practice of the staff and on the capacities and interests of the children.

In previous chapters it has been argued that, on the surface, working-class Ramsay and middle-class Fieldhouse eschewed a rigid structure. Ramsay was relatively free; Fieldhouse appeared so, but its endeavours were integrated into a less obvious structure. In both institutions there was little evidence of the 'division of labour' which obtained at Castleton, a school which was identical to Ramsay in architecture. Mrs Smith at Ramsay never mentioned her administrative burden. Her dress at work was very informal: she usually wore the same kind of uniform as her staff did. Sometimes she wore overalls. She would sit down on the floor with the children. The social distance among staff was minimal at Ramsay and all seemed very cordial.

The same could be said of Fieldhouse, where Miss Foot was teacher-in-charge. Miss Foot had virtual autonomy *vis-à-vis* the infant school. There were no formal staff meetings, only coffee breaks where ideas were exchanged informally.

Miss Foot: We just bounce ideas off each other [at coffee break].

Miss Foot took her place in the same rota of duties which her colleagues followed: she cleaned up; she made the beds (these were used to rest the children at lunchtime); she submitted the requisitions. The same informality which she displayed to her children she extended to her colleagues, as had Mrs Smith. Finally, the lack of awareness of other nurseries was an oft-repeated remark. The nursery nurses did not move; the headteachers did meet regularly; the teachers-in-charge of the nursery *units* attached to primary schools (such as Miss Foot) never met each other, and nor, curiously, did they attend the nursery *school* headteachers' meetings.

SUMMARY

This chapter has been about professional relationships in the nursery school. That is to say, it has considered the extent to which nursery schools reveal status group rivalries. Unlike the majority of schools, nursery schools contain two clearly demarcated roles: the teacher and the nursery nurse. But although, at the level of formal role-definition they differ, nevertheless, in practice, few discernible differences emerge. In some settings, the differences are remarked upon whilst in others they are not. At Castleton, the status group rivalry was for the most part contained *within* the nursery nurse staff. There was no criticism which was made obvious to the headteacher. It was, however, vented to me, the researcher, who was seen to have no stake in the organization. And although the headteacher had declared herself to be open to different opinion, some staff may have felt that there were few opportunities to give it. In part, this was due to the separate rooms in which 'nursing' and 'teaching' staff took their coffee breaks (allowing the teaching staff to answer the door and telephone), and in part it may have been due to the infrequency of staff meetings. That said, some of the nursery nurses may have felt 'trapped' at that level, both in terms of salary and formal status, and may have sought a scapegoat in the teaching staff. At Ramsay and Fieldhouse, however, formal staff meetings were few, but all strata in the hierarchy shared 'classroom' and 'staffroom' life to a high degree. The consensus was informally and continuously remade through these shared day-to-day activities.

NOTES AND REFERENCES

1. Collins, R. *The Credential Society*. New York: Academic Press, 1979.
2. Hoyle, E. 'The micropolitics of educational organizations'. *Educational Management and Administration*, **10**, 87-98, 1982; and Ball, S.J. *The Micro-Politics of the School: Towards a Theory of School Organization*. London: Methuen, 1987.
3. Scottish Education Department. *The Primary School in Scotland*. Edinburgh: HMSO, 1950, p. 129.
4. Scottish Education Department. *Before Five*. Edinburgh: HMSO, 1971, p. 46.
5. Strathclyde Regional Council. *Under Fives*. Glasgow: Strathclyde Regional Council, 1985; and Penn, H. 'The Strathclyde Pre-Fives Policy: development and debate'. *Scottish Educational Review*, **20**, 118-20, 1988.
6. Scottish Education Department. *16-18s in Scotland: An Action Plan*. Edinburgh: Scottish Education Department, 1983.

CHAPTER 10
Summary and Conclusions

This final chapter has a threefold purpose: first, to bring together the elements of the book and to attempt a summary of the main trends which the evidence has generated; second, to explain sociologically the meaning of these trends, and to discuss the explanation in relation to current issues in the sociology of early education; and third, to suggest that early education may loom large in forthcoming policy debates. Due caution is warranted in inferring generalizations from a study of only three nurseries.

The interpretative framework which informed the study drew upon Berger's concept of the 'bureaucratic cognitive style'. In respect of this, we considered the extent to which notions of *time*, *space*, *assessment*, *authority* and the *structure of activities* accorded with the Weberian ideal typical bureaucracy. In addition, the ways in which the staff themselves related to each other were also set within this concept. Our analysis suggested that the extent of bureaucratic structure is greatest at Castleton, and least at Fieldhouse and at Ramsay. This is not to say that Castleton came close to a pure bureaucracy; rather it is to say that, in relation to the other two nursery schools, it revealed more of the elements of a bureaucratic regime. The apparent similarity between Ramsay, the nursery school in the most deprived area, and Fieldhouse, which is in the most prosperous area, warrants further analysis.

In Chapter 2, 'Childhood and society', it was argued that the explanation of childhood and early education could not be reducible to theory drawn from psychology alone, even though Piagetian developmental psychology remains prominent in the theory of early education. It gives little consideration to the child in society, and in a society which itself has a history. With this in mind, the relationship to nursery education of the interplay between capitalism as a mode of production, on the one hand, and Darwinism as an influence on our ways of thinking about mind and body, on the other hand, was discussed. In respect of capitalism's influence on childhood, two points were given fuller treatment. The first was that in order to maximize the efficiency and profitability of industrial concerns, a bureaucratic form of work-based organization was deemed to be optimal. Following on from this, we considered Berger's insight that technology and bureaucracy at work have a ripple effect in that they influence our consciousness beyond the workplace and in education, thereby fostering what he calls the 'bureaucratic cognitive style'. The second influence to be derived from capitalism is its tendency to differentiate society along the lines of social classes. To these can be added two Darwinian notions: the first turns on the maxim of 'the survival of the fittest' (which gives a so-called biological basis to competitive individualism); the second emphasizes the classification and measurement of 'individual differences'.

The analysis in Chapter 2 also noted the importance of Norbert Elias's social theory for our understanding of childhood: that is, childhood emerged as a discrete cultural category during the post-medieval period, and can be seen as a consequence of increasing levels of shame among the aristocracy and bourgeoisie as society succumbed to state control and became more differentiated. Crucial to our analysis here is Elias's argument that the individual's regulation of affects is likely to occur last of all among the poor. Finally, there has occurred in post-medieval Europe an appeal to the innocence of the child: that the young child should not be deprived of his or her sensate pleasures and spontaneity in an increasingly rational and 'disenchanted' world marked by predictability and formality. This tradition has long been associated with Rousseau and Froebel. It marks an important aspect of the child-centred discourse on nursery education.

With these influences of rationality, bureaucracy, capitalism, Darwinism and romanticism in mind, let us consider the apparent similarity of the evidence which has been adduced to typify the educational theory and practice at Ramsay and Fieldhouse. The main difference between the two nurseries is the extent to which the children's activities are rendered thematic and integrated. At

Ramsay, this was little in evidence: activities tended to be discrete. Not so at Fieldhouse. Of all the nurseries, Fieldhouse exemplified Bernstein's 'invisible pedagogy', of which more in a moment. The relative lack of 'bureaucracy' at Ramsay appeared to be explained by Mrs Smith's averred concern to preserve the innocence of her children, whose domestic lives were thought to be marked by difficulty and anxiety. It was as if, too, she wished to extend their happiness before they entered the very formal world of the local primary school. Affection towards the children appeared to be a guiding maxim at Ramsay. Her one-time ability to teach them the 'basics' was increasingly being rendered more difficult by children whose speech, diet and hygiene were already 'backward'. As best she could, she gave her children freedom and emotional security in a setting devoid of threats and replete with affection. In no sense were the Ramsay children seen to be culpable; they were victims of an environment not of their making. Whether Mrs Smith thought their parents were culpable, she did not say. And nor did she offer any explanations of why, in the first place, there existed 'areas of multiple deprivation' such as that which served as the catchment area for her school. Ramsay came closest to Rousseau's vision of childhood. More than elsewhere, childhood was regarded there as an end in itself, complete and natural, and not as a deficient form of adulthood.

Fieldhouse also seemed to be relatively informal. Here was a nursery which virtually assaulted the eyes with its vibrant art and craft displays. It appeared to be very free. Nobody was caressed or cajoled. The children behaved with a degree of self-control that would have marked them out as very mature had they been at Castleton or Ramsay. They appeared to be both free and purposeful, unstructured yet structured. In short, much of their behaviour seemed to be that of the assured adult. Their activities, however, were highly integrated. In short, they were being 'taught' both *self-control* and *relationships between activities and objects*. They personified — albeit in an embryonic stage — the degree of affect regulation and sense of 'otherhood' which Elias has pointed to in a society marked by complexity of purpose. For here was 'soft' bureaucracy: a more human relations management style suited to life in the professions in the service sector, what Bernstein has termed the 'new middle class'.[1] But what is interesting about Fieldhouse is that, at one and the same time, it appears to express the long-heralded romanticism of child-centredness *and* to anticipate the managerial regimes of life in the professions. Both romanticism and industrialism are apparently well served by it. Here there was no notion of protection and innocence of the kind advocated at Ramsay; rather, self-confidence and sophistication were to be observed and encouraged. Whereas the staff at Ramsay sought to extend the innocence of childhood, at Fieldhouse it was if anything being reduced.

Castleton did not seem to have the certainty of purpose observed at either Fieldhouse or Ramsay. At Castleton, a sense of dilemma seemed evident. On the one hand, the headteacher alluded much to caring and to child-centredness. Like Mrs Smith at Ramsay, Mrs Chalmers at Castleton worked with deprived children, though not as many, and not as deprived. These formed a nursery-within-a-nursery, being housed in the 'full-time room' under Mrs Turner, who would have had much in common with Ramsay's Mrs Smith. They had to deal with the same kind of children and they behaved in the same way towards them. Mrs Chalmers saw all of her children, not just these 'full-time' children, and her declared purpose was educational, in the academic sense. Here she was not at one with Mrs Turner, whose purpose was predicated on sympathy and affection, and who found the goings-on beyond the 'full-time room' to be too formal and structured. In the 'areas', however, conditions were crowded, much more so than either in the 'full-time' room or in Ramsay nursery, where attendance rates were lower, therefore leaving more space. Part of the reason for the greater formality in the 'areas' at Castleton may have been the fact that it was simply more populated. On the other hand, Mrs Chalmers wished to provide her children with a certain 'readiness' for school which would stand them in good stead, and which might therefore enable them to 'make something of themselves'. Here she echoed the sentiments of Project Head Start, namely that the War on Poverty, to use President Johnson's phrase, can be fought and won in the nursery school. Her analysis partly anticipated Tizard *et al.*'s recent findings in London. In their study of working-class infant schools in inner London, they found that the best predictor of academic attainment at the end of infant schooling is the level of attainment at the end of nursery schooling. Despite this, the sample of nursery teachers whom Tizard interviewed did not, in the main, set much emphasis on '3R knowledge'.[2] To return to Mrs Chalmers: as she put it, she 'knowingly tried to get the best' for her children, in both a caring and academic sense. But child-centred romanticism was not easily reconcilable with meritocratic individualism. In the presence of children from 'difficult' backgrounds, she may have had academic aspirations for them which her staff could not wholly share, and this may have generated an undercurrent of tension.

To summarize: in two of the nurseries there appears to be a clear provision for the imperatives of capitalism and child-centred educational philosophy. First, as stated, the *apparent* freedom assigned to the children at 'new' middle-class Fieldhouse squares with this philosophy *and* provides anticipatory socialization for the children of the professional parent in the service sector; second, at Ramsay, the regime is equally functional for capitalism and also accords with the child-centred rhetoric. It is functional for capitalism in that, by protecting the children, Ramsay is less concerned with the 'cognitive outcomes' which would constitute a set of sound 'basics' for school and academic success within it. Even by the nursery's own admission, the children were at least a year behind on entering primary school *as compared with other working-class area nurseries*. Through no fault of their own, the staff had to teach children the 'basics' which those in most other nurseries could take as given. It might have been the private view of the staff at Ramsay that few of their children would make it anyway, so why should all of them be 'stretched', thereby possibly causing the children more anguish than that which they already faced at home? Thus, even though the 'protectionist' policy at Ramsay was extremely well-intentioned and humanitarian (and therefore appealed to romantic educational philosophy), nevertheless it was *unintentionally* functional for preserving these children in the lower echelons of the working class. The headteacher at the other working-class nursery, Mrs Chalmers, may have tried to steer a course between meritocracy and romanticism, but settled for the former tack, perhaps to the dismay (or even bewilderment) of some of her staff.

How does this analysis relate to the sociology of early education? In Chapter 2, it was noted that Bernstein has speculated that 'new' middle-class parents may influence the pedagogy of infant education so that the forms of pedagogy and control in the home accord with those in the school.[3] This pedagogy he terms the 'invisible' pedagogy. Previous studies of infant classrooms in primary schools have failed to find evidence of it.[4] In the study here, the school which best accords with Bernstein's 'new' middle class, Fieldhouse, has much which could be seen as 'invisible' pedagogy. As to the sociological explanation of the 'invisible' pedagogy in 'new' middle-class nurseries and infant schools (assuming such were to be the case), a number of strands can be adduced.

Bernstein's explanation turns on the relationship between the changing modes of control in the work settings of the emergent service sector economy, particularly at the professional and managerial levels, where high degrees of social and communication skills are required. Here, therefore, pedagogical change reflects technical change. Marxist critics of Bernstein have argued that the invisible pedagogy is functional not simply for technical considerations, but for those who own that technology, namely capitalists. To say that technology *per se* is the explanation is to ignore the crucial question of who benefits from it, and from any changes in pedagogy which arise out of it. Elias would argue that both Bernstein and the Marxists are grappling with only part of the explanation: first, the trend towards the self-regulation of impulses implied by the 'invisible' pedagogy has long anticipated both capitalism and the technical changes to which both Marxists and Bernstein respectively allude. Second, Elias argued that this kind of affect control descends the social order, and this would explain why Fieldhouse would be first to experience it. Added to this, Marxists try to explain the social order, and for them the explanation is capitalism. Hierarchy, however, is not the sole preserve of capitalist societies, as Weber argued. It, and the increasing degree of what Elias has called the 'web of interconnectedness' are functions of modernity.[5] However, the 'bureaucratic cognitive style' analysed by Berger may become 'softened' as the human relations management style comes to suffuse the service sector of advanced industrial societies, be they capitalist or socialist. To this end, therefore, there may be an increasing convergence in early education of a mutually reinforcing set of influences emanating from the long-entrenched philosophy of romanticism and the newly emergent 'real world' needs of industrialism. The 'soft' bureaucracy of the nursery school and the identities it structures will serve to satisfy both.

What of the immediate future for pre-compulsory education? Will it become compulsory, thereby marking a further institutional imposition on childhood? There are indications that it might. First, since 1979, higher, further, secondary and primary education have all been reformed. Only pre-school provision has escaped. Its turn may have come. Second, to the trained bureaucratic eye, pre-school provision lacks organizational elegance. It is a mess, with a diversity of provision and institutional labels. It is ripe for rationalization. Third, and linked to the latter, is the tendency for bureaucracies to engage in empire-building, so as to insulate themselves from predators. Pre-school provision may provide a unique opportunity for government social work services to expand. (It is a situation partly analogous to the relationship between the Manpower Services Commission and non-advanced further education in the mid-1980s.) Indeed, there are already, in the Strathclyde Region in Scotland, signs of the impending contest. In addition, recent shifts in Britain towards a national curriculum, with legislated content (though not in Scotland), raise the question of whether or not 5-year-olds are ready for it, in so far as the 'basics' are concerned. In order to ensure this, guidelines may be issued to nursery schools. This, too, would have the added tactical benefit to the Scottish Office Education Department and the Department of Education and Science of defining pre-school provision in *academic* terms, not those of nursing and caring. It would then be difficult for social work services to legitimate their interest in pre-five provision. But the most compelling reason for the expansion of pre-school education may turn out to be economic. As the proportion of the post-16 workforce shrinks, women with children may be encouraged to return to waged work, and pre-school provision will be required. Ideologically, the Conservative government might prefer to leave this provision to the private sector, to employers. On the other hand, if state provision can maximize the gross national product (by permitting women to work), then it may be a price worth paying.

Finally, it was suggested at the beginning of the book that its intention was analytical, neither prescriptive nor purportedly practical. This is not to say that practical implications cannot be drawn. If the earlier speculation about the impending policy focus on early education proves to be correct, then those involved in early education will be either part of, or witnesses to, the debate. If tradition is followed, we can expect the policy initiatives to be couched in democratic-sounding terminology, replete with references to the needs of the individual. All this will resonate well with the existing repertoire of concepts used by nursery educators. The discourse of developmental psychology and individualism will fuse together. But this will leave out of account the fact that early education is a social endeavour, with social and political effects at the societal level. Understandably, nursery educators must deal practically with the here-and-now of their children in their nursery. It is a demanding occupation, one which leaves little time for reflecting critically on the aggregative effects of nursery education as a whole. At best, questions raised in nurseries are 'how' questions about practical issues. The deeper 'why' questions about nursery education are omitted. Similarly, in-service provision seeks to answer the former, to omit the latter. As in the education of children, so in that of teachers, it is the knowledge which is omitted which is often crucial. Unless the education of those involved in early education moves beyond its present preoccupation with psychology, it will limit their capacity to engage fully in the policy debates to come.

NOTES AND REFERENCES

1. Bernstein, B. 'Class and pedagogies: visible and invisible' (1975). In Bernstein, B. *Class, Codes and Control*, Volume III. 2nd edition. London: Routledge & Kegan Paul, 1977.
2. Tizard, B., Blatchford, P., Burke, J., Farquhar, C. and Plewis, I. *Young Children at School in the Inner City*. Hove: Lawrence Erlbaum Associates, pp. 168–9, 1988.

3. Bernstein, op. cit. (1).

4. Hartley, D. 'Some consequences of teachers' definitions of boys and girls in two infant schools'. Exeter: Unpublished PhD thesis, University of Exeter, 1977; and King, R. 'In search of the invisible pedagogy'. *Sociology*, **13**, 445–58, 1979.

5. Berger, P., Berger, B. and Kellner, H. *The Homeless Mind*. Harmondsworth: Penguin, 1973.

Response

In November 1987 I sent a full draft of the book to the nurseries, inviting their reactions, reminding them that my purpose had been neither criticism nor evaluation, and noting that the book depicted policies and practices which may not reflect current ones. I intimated that I would contact each school in January 1988 in order to discuss their comments on the draft. In early February it was made known to me that the staff of all the schools and units would prefer to meet me *en masse*. To this I agreed, although I would have preferred to have seen the staff in smaller groups. In turn, I asked if they would permit the presence of a colleague who would provide me with notes of the meeting. They agreed.

In my introduction to the meeting, I discussed briefly the substance of the history of childhood. In particular, I explained how my use of the term 'bureaucratic' was for analytical purposes, and that no evaluative connotation was intended. With the use of slides, I gave a summary of the research.

As the meeting progressed, it became clear that the book had been interpreted in two ways. First, as I had suspected, some participants had tended to focus only on the parts which they believed to refer to themselves as individuals. Second, the staff of the three nurseries had informally rated themselves against what they perceived to be the official wisdom on nursery education. One participant stated that I had listened to 'tittle-tattle'. As to the second interpretation, two of the schools appeared to think that they had accorded with official practice; another, less so. It was especially noticeable that very few of the nursery nurses said anything at the meeting. Some did so afterwards, privately. Aside from minor matters of fact, two nurseries agreed with the data; the third requested a subsequent meeting to clarify matters privately. Errors of fact were corrected, as were some of interpretation. I agreed to paraphrase some verbatim quotations, while keeping their meaning. I was informed that in one of the schools, the draft had produced a short-lived escalation in the micro-politics of the school. In short, my overall analysis was retained, and in two of the schools my evidence was perhaps not as rich as it might have been. At the end of the day, I seemed to have unwittingly heeded the comment of one participant at the meeting: 'It [the draft] should not be tampered with; it might be tempered a little.'

One of the outcomes of the main meeting was that the line of communication between the regional directorate (which had arranged my access to the schools) and the staff, particularly the nursery nurses, had become attenuated. I gathered that the nurseries had felt obliged to participate in some instances. I was advised, too, that in future a 'contract' would be agreed, according to a specification. Ironically, this would serve to set research in the very mould of the bureaucratic cognitive style to which I have been referring throughout the book. It was also put to me that I had not used impersonal numbers to identify staff, as had been the case in the study held up to me as an example of this type of research. I pointed out that the study in question had been of over 200 teachers, and that the researchers had set out to gather many pieces of data from structured observation schedules and questionnaires. An unintended consequence of the meeting was that it proved to be the first time that all levels of the nursery hierarchy had sat around a table to discuss a piece of research about their nurseries in particular, and about nursery education in general. Increasingly, as teacher appraisal looms large, outsiders will raise questions on the theory and practice of nursery education. Evaluations will be made, and they will have official sanction. Unless nursery teachers and nursery nurses are well prepared for these interventions and evaluations of their work, the official wisdom of the appraisers — their criteria and their performance indicators — will go uncontested. An outside researcher, with no stake in the hierarchy of nursery education, can provide a stimulus to debate. One of the most gratifying aspects of the discussion of the research was the opportunity for staff to take up positions about individuals and ideas in nursery schools. They did so with energy and eloquence.

Timetables

II.1 Ramsay, Castleton and Fieldhouse: Mornings

RAMSAY

09.00–09.20	Registration and badges
09.20–09.55	Free play in different areas
09.55–10.00	Tidy-up time
10.00–10.10	Staff tea-break/snack-time
10.10–10.20	as above
10.20–10.55	Free play
10.55–11.00	Tidy-up time
11.00–11.15	Story time
11.15–11.30	Going-home time

CASTLETON

09.00–09.45	Free play, Wendy House, sand, water, large apparatus, table games, baking
09.45–10.00	Juice-time, conversation
10.00–10.10	Staff tea-break
10.10–10.20	Staff tea-break
10.30–10.45	Free play, in or out
10.45–11.00	Outdoor play, or singing or games (movement or music)
11.00–11.15	Story time
11.15–11.20	Distribution of paintings, craftwork, library books
11.20–11.30	Departure

FIELDHOUSE

09.00–09.20	Registration (no badges)
09.20–09.55	Thematic activities, play

09.55–10.00	Tidy-up time
10.00–10.20	Snack-time, singing, drama
10.20–11.15	Thematic activities, free play
11.15–11.20	Distribution of work, books
11.20–11.30	Departure

Assessment Checklists

III.1 Ramsay

Sight:
All right
Glasses
Squint

Hearing:
All right
Impaired

Dominant hand:
Right
Left

Holds pencil correctly
Draws simple human figures

Walking normal
Running
Skipping
Climbing
Accident-prone
Very active

SELF-MANAGEMENT
Coat (puts on/fastens)
Shoes (puts on/fastens)
Cares for self and others
Washes hands
Manages fastenings

SOCIAL PLAY
Solitary
Co-operative
Parallel

MANIPULATIVE PLAY
Block building:
Vertical
Horizontal

Screws
Strings beads
Uses scissors

COGNITIVE
Looks at books
Listens to stories
Retells stories
Discusses experiences
Knows parts of the body
Can tell own name
Names simple objects
Can tell own address
Follows instructions
Can count to five
Can identify 1 to 5
Can copy shapes
Can name shapes
Circle, square, triangle
Can name colours

LANGUAGE
Speaks plainly
Uses single words
Uses phrases
Uses sentences

EMOTIONAL
Temper tantrums
Aggressive

Timorous
Outgoing
Attention-seeking

RELATIONSHIP WITH
ADULTS
Friendly
Withdrawn

Name Index

Anyon, J. 36, 42
Aries, P. 7
Armstrong, M. 36, 41
Aya, R. 30, 31

Ball, S.J. 42, 140
Banet, B. 74
Bantock, G.H. 31
Barrie, J.M. 89
Bentham, Jeremy 76, 93
Berger, B. 32, 41, 74, 117, 127, 128, 149
Berger, P. 1, 18, 32, 35, 38, 41, 42, 74, 94, 117, 127, 128, 141, 146, 149
Berlak, A. 36, 42
Berlak, H. 36, 42
Bernstein, B. 26–8, 30, 33, 36, 41, 42, 91, 121, 128, 144, 146, 148
Bidwell, C.E. 74, 93
Blatchford, P. 4, 148
Bourdieu, P. 30
Brass, D.J. 93
Bronfenbrenner, U. 25
Brown, G. 56
Buckle, H.T. 34
Buck-Morss, S. 14, 31, 32, 59, 74
Bureau of Labor Statistics 62
Burke, J. 4, 148

Callahan, R.E. 24
Carroll, Lewis 23
Casa, Giovanni della 11
Collins, R. 140
Cook, R. 56
Crabtree, M. 22

Darling, J. 118
David, T. 93
Douglas, M. 32, 46
Durkheim, E. 26, 31

Elias, N. 3, 5, 8–13, 30, 31, 32, 39, 58, 59, 61, 74, 120, 128, 142, 143, 146
Entwistle, H. 32
Erasmus 11–12, 19

Farquhar, C. 4, 148
Farquharson, E. 34
Flanders, N.A. 41
Foucault, M. 116, 118
Freire, P. 34
Freud, Sigmund 44
Froebel, F. 24–5, 33, 119, 142

157

Name Index

Galton, F. 20
Gibson, R. 32
Glaser, B. 42
Goffman, E. 88, 93
Gregory, S. 128

Hall, E.T. 75, 93
Hamilton, D. 32, 93
Hartley, David (1705–1757) 21-2
Hartley, D. 33, 34, 36, 41, 42,
    128, 148
Hedge, A. 93
Her Majesty's Inspectorate 52
Hobson, J.A. 74
Hohmann, M. 74
Hoyle, E. 140
Humes, W. 93

Ingleby, D. 33, 128
Isaacs, S. 104, 118

Jacobson, L. 128
James, A. 7, 30
Johnson, Lyndon B. 144

Kanter, R. 28, 33, 36, 41
Kellner, H. 32, 41, 74, 117, 149
King, R. 27, 33, 36, 41, 42, 149
Kuzmics, H. 32

Locke, John 15-17, 19, 21, 115,
    118

Lowndes, G.A.N. 56
Lubeck, S. 28, 33, 36, 41, 74
Luchaire, A. 10, 31
Luckmann, T. 42

McMillan, M. 2, 53, 84
McMillan, R. 2, 84
Makins, V. 74, 118
Mehan, H. 117
Meyrowitz, J. 8, 30
Milbank, J.E. 3, 4
Montessori, M. 103, 117

Nasaw, D. 32
Neill, S.R. St. J. 93
Newson, E. 128
Newson, J. 128
Nias, J. 36, 42
Nisbet, J. 33
Notestein, W. 34

Oldham, G.R. 93
Opie, I. 8, 30
Opie, P. 8, 30
Osborn, A.F. 3, 4
Owen, Robert 22, 32

Parsons, T. 9
Passeron, J.C. 30
Penn, H. 140
Piaget, J. 2, 24, 25
Plewis, I. 4, 128

158

Subject Index